Must Walls Divide?

The Creative Witness of the Churches in Europe

James E. Will

Friendship Press • New York

Photo Credits

P.11 (Top) Royal Norwegian Embassy Information Service
     (Bottom) New York Public Library
P.23 New York Public Library Picture Collection
P.31 World Council of Churches
P.47 Religious News Service
P.55 National Lutheran Council News
P.78 (Top) courtesy of Polish Tourist Office
     (Bottom) courtesy of Romanian Tourist Office
P.89 Church World Service
P.99 UPCUSA
P.109 National Lutheran Council News

Library of Congress Cataloging in Publication Data

Will, James E.
   Must walls divide?

   Includes bibliographical references.
   1. Christianity — Europe. I. Title.
BR735.W54   274'.082   81-2257
ISBN 0-377-00106-6   AACR2

Editorial Offices: 475 Riverside Drive, New York, NY 10115
Distribution Office: P.O. Box 37844, Cincinnati, OH 45237

Contents

Contents

Foreword

"In Europe," he said, eyeing me keenly from under his brows, his hands clasped on his desk before him, "ecumenical work is much more difficult than anywhere else in the world." I listened carefully—for if anyone were an expert in this subject it was surely the speaker. My mentor was Dr. Willem A. Visser't Hooft. At that time—1959—he was general secretary of the World Council of Churches, and I was a new member of his staff, being briefed for a first visit to the churches in a country in East Europe. Since then, my responsibilities, first with the World Council of Churches and later with the Conference of European Churches, have kept me traveling constantly throughout the whole of Europe for over two decades. This has afforded me ample opportunity to cull material for reflection from my own experiences. A few monthis ago I had again the always profitable experience of exchanging notes with "Wim" Visser't Hooft, now honorary president of the World Council of Churches. I reminded him of his earlier remark. He said that he saw no reason for revising his judgment of 1959. And my own experience provided ample confirmation.

I mention this incident at the beginning of the introduction to a book on the dimensions of mission in Europe, for the judgment is surely apposite. If the basis of the ecumenical movement is the thrust of mission and service—and I am firmly convinced it is—then we have here a key statement about mission in Europe to which we must be attentive. There are numerous dimensions of mission in Europe, and whilst mission almost anywhere in the world is hardly ever easy, in this "little appendage to the landmass of Asia," as someone has

1

disdainfully described Europe, the inescapable task of the Christian churches and believers is especially difficult.

One could truthfully, but perhaps too generally, sum it all up by saying that into this smallest but one of all the continents there is crammed a greater degree of complexity than is found elsewhere. This is related to the fact that Europe has a relatively greater number of Christian believers (more or less active) per square mile than any other continent. But there are many other elements—historical and contemporary, doctrinal and ecclesiological, ethnic and linguistic, social and political. Within the very limited space available, and by using the method of examples rather than that of exhaustive description, the book that follows draws a remarkably stimulating picture of a total situation of variety and difference producing great complexity ... and sometimes confusion.

The method of working from examples means, quite naturally, that some elements of the situation (possibly even important ones) are not mentioned. There is a positive side to that, of course. For it means that further investigation of the subject is likely to be all the more profitable. It would be fatuous and irresponsible for the writer of an introduction even to try "to complete the picture." But perhaps two or three general observations may be permitted him, as a small addition to the wealth of information and observation contained in the book itself.

The first observation has to do with a fact of history which finds mention in the following pages—the phenomenon of "Constantinianism" (see Chapter 1, section on "Variety of Church-State Relations"). Now Europe is the only continent where, in one way or another, every country, at some period of its history, has passed through this experience. Today, of course, the situation presents us with a variety of degrees of separation between church and state. With the exception of the Scandinavian churches, the remnants of Constantinian structures are fragmentary, to say the least. But the fact remains that, at some stage in history, certain churches have been the objects of special favor on the part of the state. That, together with other historical accretions, can lead to a persistent kind of ecclesiastical superiority complex, which complicates psychologically and practically any joint effort in mission.

A second observation is related to the ties between church and culture in different parts of Europe. In general terms it is true to claim that, throughout the vicissitudes of history in the period covered by

Anni Domini, the Christian churches have been powerful inspirers of cultural activity and tenacious guardians of the cultural heritage. Political, economic and social structures have changed and will change further. The churches are being pushed steadily to the edge of society in many countries—but the basic culture and moral principles, even of those countries whose official stance is secular or frankly atheistic, remains that inspired by the now increasingly deprivileged churches. This creates major internal tensions, particularly in those churches that look back on long histories, and requires of them a particularly serious effort at adaptation. And this inevitably impinges on the understanding of mission.

In the third place, it is perhaps worthwhile to stress the fact that, although there are considerable differences in practical circumstances, it can be argued validly that the churches in all parts of Europe are facing the same basic challenge. North, south, east and west, the secularization of modern peoples is either actively corroding the church or simply ignoring its existence. The challenge, whether active or passive—and this is important to note—is fundamentally of the same nature. One significant difference is that in the socialist countries of Eastern Europe its derivation may be traced substantially to an official atheistic ideology. In the other countries it takes the form of sheer indifference on the part of the majority. It is a moot point as to which presents the more insidious kind of challenge to Christian mission.

Fourth, there is a question which has to do with dimension in a strictly statistical and organizational sense. It is widely agreed that mission only has sense if it is an ecumenical undertaking. But how do churches whose memberships are counted in millions really get down to this task together with those whose memberships are counted in tens of thousands? Within the restricted national confines of Europe this is often an acute problem. The elephant and the mouse have never had too easy a time of it in closely confined quarters!

Dr. Will is to be highly commended on the conviction so clearly stated in the first sentence of his preface—and on his outstanding effort toward its fulfillment. Europe as a whole! A standard to be set by all who would endeavor to appreciate the dimensions of mission in this continent. Perhaps it is an ideal impossible to attain. But the effort to achieve such a view will at least obviate the futile expenditure of unneeded pity and sympathy on those in some situation unfamiliar to the majority of readers of this book, and sometimes exploited for political ends. May it go further and lead to the practice of those Christian virtues of which churches and believers in all parts of Europe need to be recipients ... understanding, confidence and trust.

Geneva, 13th October, 1980　　　　　**Glen Garfield Williams**
General Secretary
Conference of European Churches

Preface

In this study we intend to see Europe and its churches whole. A valuable but difficult task, with European culture wonderfully rich, yet so long divided and presently so diverse. The effort to understand it would not be worth the difficulty if the result weren't so important.

Social and religious divisions between Eastern and Western Europe go back to Constantine's relocation of the imperial capital from Rome to Constantinople in 330 A.D. They have been strongly reinforced by the political blocs dividing east and west—"communist" and "free"—since World War II. For many North Americans, all too accustomed to a tragic reduction that permits the west to name itself as if it were the whole, Europe has shrunk to the dimensions of Western Europe.[1] Newspapers regularly inform us of the *"European* Economic Community,"* so named though made up of only nine *west* European states. The *"European* Parliament" convenes in Strasbourg with delegates elected only from ten states in *Western* Europe.

In spite of religious anathemas 1,000 years old and contemporary political conflicts, Europe still is constituted by both its eastern and western halves. It makes little geographical, cultural or religious sense to set the boundary of Europe anywhere west of the Ural Mountains in the Soviet Union. The Letts and Slavs of the east—later the Bulgars and Magyars—belong as surely to Europe as the Celts, Nordic and Germanic peoples of the west or the Greeks and Romans of the south. The cultural and religious histories of all peoples inhabiting the European peninsula that stretches 3,300 miles from Asia to the Atlantic Ocean constitute an interacting whole. Even the

5

two million square miles of European Russia are still Europe.

Neither the history nor the contemporary mission of European churches can be understood unless their continent is given these dimensions. Central to their mission is seeking to bring peace to ancient antagonisms, healing to long-standing divisions that run through Europe and extend to our own shores. The European origin of most of our North American population has brought almost all of Europe's ethnic, national and religious divisions to our society. The wounds of its present ideological divisions are irritated by continuing concerns for human rights and "captive nations."

Though we intend to see Europe whole, that does not mean seeing it as *the* whole. The long tradition of identifying Christian faith and Europe is summed up in Hilaire Belloc's epigram, "The faith is Europe, and Europe is the faith."[2] It may be true that as Europe was Christianized, Christianity was Europeanized, but that is not the whole truth. The twentieth-century theologian Ernst Troeltsch (1865-1923) was wrong in concluding that Christianity is essentially the fulfillment of European aspirations and that Jesus Christ can function redemptively only for modern Europeans.

We must not see Europe as "the whole" because the contemporary mission of European churches includes the liberation and development of peoples colonized by Europeans during the last five centuries. Beginning in the sixteenth century, European nations developed a technological and military superiority that allowed them to reduce much of Africa, Asia and South America to subservience. Restructuring these relations of "domination and dependence"[3] in terms of justice and interdependence is a crucial mission of contemporary European churches.

In the twentieth century almost all of the Christian churches in Europe have responded to the ecumenical call to achieve "visible unity in one faith," as the constitution of the World Council of Churches puts it. They are gathered into their own regional Conference of European Churches, as well as the World Council of Churches. Though it remains difficult, it has become possible to study the mission of European churches as a whole, while not confusing Europe with the whole *oikumene*.

This study should make it possible for North American Christians to have a more concrete ecumenical relation with all their sisters and brothers ecclesiastically related to:
• Pimen, Patriarch of Moscow and all Russia;

- Demetrios I, Ecumenical Patriarch in Istanbul;
- John Paul II, Bishop of Rome and Pope of the Roman Catholic Church;
- Albrecht Schönherr, Bishop of the Evangelical Church of Berlin-Brandenburg and President of the Federation of Evangelical Churches in the German Democratic Republic;
- Herman Sticher, Bishop of the Evangelical Methodist Church in the Federal Republic of Germany;
- Max-Alain Chevallier, President of the National Council of the Reformed Church of France;
- Inga Bengtzon of Sweden, President of Diakonia, the World Federation of Deaconess Associations;
- Robert Runcie, Archbishop of Canterbury;
- as well as many other sisters and brothers in Jesus Christ.

Knowing and loving them more, we may understand better some dimensions of their contemporary mission, and perhaps also our own.

1. The Variety and Vitality of Church Life in Europe

Historical Introduction and Overview

For most of its history, Christianity has been primarily a European religion. The cultural history of all European peoples is intimately interrelated with the histories of their churches. Neither the Roman Catholic Church nor the cultures of France, Spain, Italy, Austria, Hungary, Poland and Lithuania can be understood apart from each other. The same is true of Greece, Serbia, Romania, Bulgaria and Russia when apart from the history of the Orthodox churches. The cultures of central and northwestern Europe—Germany, Scandinavia, the Netherlands, England and Scotland—have been profoundly interrelated with the history of the Reformation since the sixteenth century.[1]

The conflicts of European history inevitably have had a religious component. The great schism of 1054 between Roman Catholicism and Eastern Orthodoxy explains some of the tensions between Serbians and Croatians in Yugoslavia today, and Poles and Lithuanians vis-a-vis the Russians in Eastern Europe. The bitter conflicts of the Reformation left their imprint on the religiously pluralistic Central European countries of Hungary, Czechoslovakia, Germany and Switzerland and are perpetuated in the continuing tragedy of Northern Ireland. The fact that Islam once challenged the Orthodox churches in every Balkan country explains many continuing anxieties in Yugoslavia, the hostility between Greece and Turkey, and the unresolved conflict in Cyprus.

The real unity of European culture also cannot be understood apart from the ecumenical reality of the churches. Building on the great achievement of the Romans, the Catholic Church succeeded in holding most Western European peoples culturally together after the Roman Empire dissolved. The unity created by the Holy Roman Empire prior to our modern nation states has not yet been entirely dissolved by the acids of modern nationalism. The present unity of Eastern Europe derives in part from the Dukes of Moscow of the sixteenth century thinking of Moscow as the "Third Rome" and inheritor of the destiny that the imperial Christian centers of Rome and Constantinople had carried.

Variety and Vitality of the Churches

Our principal concern is the contemporary variety and vitality of European churches. The brief historical sketch above outlines some of the variety. It is important, however, to appreciate the vitality the Holy Spirit brings to the life of these churches.

Because most North Americans know so little about the churches in Eastern Europe we will concentrate most of our attention there. Some suffer under the delusion that they have only a precarious "underground" existence on the edge of extinction. Though tragically true in communist Albania, it is an ideological illusion where the rest of Eastern Europe is concerned. Many eastern churches have been severely restricted, first by Islam, and by communist governments in our century. Sometimes they have suffered direct persecution. Nevertheless, the contemporary churches of Eastern Europe exhibit strong vitality, evidenced by the significantly greater proportion of the population that regularly worships in Christian congregations as compared to Western Europe. Far from leading to their demise, the challenges eastern churches have had to meet have contributed to their strength.

Lack of information and perspective on East European churches in North America is due to three factors: (1) the ideological split between east and west, (2) the structure of overseas ministries which continues to relate North American churches primarily to areas where they have sent missionaries, and (3) the fact that a large number of

Two examples of the diversity of church architecture in medieval Europe.
(Top) Urnes Stave Church, Norway. (Bottom) Montmajour Abbey, France.

Christians in Eastern Europe are Orthodox, while only a small percentage of North American Christians are.

Orthodoxy

Orthodoxy, the tradition that most North Americans know least, forms the major churches in Armenia, Georgia, Russia and the Ukraine in the Soviet Union, Serbia in Yugoslavia, and the whole of Bulgaria, Romania and Greece. All but Greece are communist states. Only Greece and Yugoslavia are not part of eastern bloc economic and military structures. Orthodoxy also has minor but significant churches in Poland and Czechoslovakia.

Despite the political upheavals in this area during the last 500 years, these churches were originally and endurably shaped during a period of almost unbelievable political stability. The Eastern Empire endured for 1,000 years, beginning in the fifth century and ending in 1453 when Constantinople fell to Turkish Muslims. Orthodox Christians still regard as normative the holy tradition that was confirmed in the fifth (553), sixth (680-1) and seventh (787) ecumenical councils. They believe that this living tradition mediates the true spirituality of Jesus Christ. Though new ecumenical councils might augment this holy tradition, any revision by any body short of an ecumenical council is immediately suspect. These are churches that value continuity and expect to be sustained through whatever temporary challenges befall them.[2]

The national churches of modern Eastern Orthodoxy both sustain and are sustained by this continuous tradition. Among them, the Moscow Patriarchate of the Russian Orthodox Church sees itself as having inherited the destiny of Rome and Constantinople after they fell as universal Christian centers. This "Third Rome," though chastened by the communist revolution, still safeguards the orthodox tradition in the twentieth century.

During the 60 years it has lived within a state led by a militantly atheistic political party, the Russian Orthodox Church's institutional strength has been severely, sometimes brutally, curtailed. It has perhaps one-fifth the clergy it had in 1914 prior to the revolution—10,000 in comparison to 50,000. There are only about 7,500 out of more than 54,000 churches left. Theological seminaries have been reduced from 57 to three and theological academies for advanced studies, from four to two.

No accurate statistics of the total number of faithful in the population have been kept by either church or state since Stalin threw out the census of 1937. He required that it be taken again in 1939 without religious questions, probably because of his displeasure that the 1937 census showed so large a percentage of believers still present in the Soviet population. Most estimate that there are 30-50 million faithful in the Russian Orthodox Church out of a population of roughly 170 million Russians, Ukrainians and Byellorussians in the Soviet Union. Some estimates are much larger. To this must be added the Armenian Gregorian National Church centered in Etschmaizine, which includes perhaps 70 percent of the 2.5 million people in the Armenian Republic, and the considerable strength of the Georgian Orthodox Church, centered in Tbilissi.

The decline of the practice of religion in European Russia is due more to persecution and the general secularization of urbanized and industrialized European culture than to the success of atheist propaganda. The atheism taught in the schools and propagated by the "League of the Militant Godless" in the 1930s and the "Scientific Atheist Section" of the All-Union Society for the Dissemination of Scientific and Political Knowledge since 1947 is relatively wooden. For many sensitive youth and adults with the opportunity to compare, it is no match for the profundity and beauty of the Orthodox tradition and liturgy. Unfortunately, state power still denies many such an opportunity.[3]

Orthodox theology is primarily concerned for salvation in the glory of the God relation. It is always closely related to the liturgical life of the people. The spiritual community at worship participates symbolically in the community of the divine trinity. Anyone privileged to take part in Russian Orthodox worship marvels at the deep devotion its congregations express.

Prior to their experience in a communist state, the Orthodox Churches of Bulgaria and Romania endured the trial of safeguarding the faith and culture of their people during four centuries of Muslim rule. The result for both was the union of national and religious loyalties in a way that no state can hope to sever, at least in the foreseeable future.

Romania continues to have approximately 85 percent, of a population of more than 20 million, who regard themselves as Orthodox. The church serves them in more than 8,000 parishes with almost 12,000 church and chapel buildings and 114 monastic houses. There are approximately 10,000 priests, 1,500 nuns and 600 monks. They are trained in six seminaries with more than 1,500 students and two institutes of university status with 1,500 students. Of the 15 percent non-Orthodox in Romania, 12 percent are Catholic and Protestant, with fewer than 3 percent claiming no religious confession. More about the mission of The Romanian Orthodox Church is included in Chapter 3.

The Orthodox Church in Bulgaria, though a strong spiritual community, is smaller in relation to its population. Out of 8.5 million in 1971, it counts about 6 million baptized, who are served in 2,600 parishes by 1,500 priests and 400 monks and nuns. Unlike Romania, there is a distinct shortage of clergy, but 200 students are presently in preparation in one theological seminary and 120 in the theological academy in Sofia. The numbers of Catholics and Protestants are very small but about 800,000 Muslims remain in Bulgaria. In an interesting statistic that emerged in the surveys of religious belief by the "Section For Historical Materialism" of the Institute of Philosophy of the Bulgarian Academy of Science, the percentage of the population identifying themselves as "believers" was 35.51 percent in 1962, declined to 33.06 percent in 1968, but *increased* to 48.00 percent in 1972.[4]

The Serbian Orthodox Church in Yugoslavia results from the union in 1920 of five independent churches created in the nineteenth century in the areas not subject to Turkish Muslim rule. In 1950, after the church had suffered as many as 700,000 killed by the fascist authorities of Croatia during World War II, there were about 7.5 million faithful in 2,864 parishes served by 3,100 priests. Their heroic struggle then and since has won the church high moral prestige among its people.

The Orthodox Church in Greece is the only one in Europe not now in a communist state. It has been recognized as self-governing (autocephalous) since 1850 when it decided that the ecumenical patriarch in Istanbul was too subject to Turkish control. The Greek church is noted for its large number of lay theologians, many of them graduates from the theological faculties of the universities of Athens and Thessalonica. The majority of professors of theology and many preachers in Greece are laymen. Some work through *Zoe* (Life), an association whose members edit many publications and lead a variety of Christian Unions—Men of Science, Students, Teachers, and Young Workers. The Greek Church counts more than eight million faithful in 81 dioceses.

Roman Catholic, Protestant and Anglican Churches

We will be briefer about these three traditions. Constituting the major traditions of the West, they are so much better known to us.

After Rome fell in the fifth century A.D., both church and society in the West required a new center of legitimation, power and order. The Roman papacy developed to meet that need. From the earliest period, the Bishop of Rome had been honored as first among equals in the ancient patriarchal dioceses. In the chaos after the empire's fall, however, he began to exercise power over other bishops and some- times kings as well. Late in the sixth century, Pope Gregory the Great successfully joined the material resources of the estates bequeathed to the church by the rich Roman families that had fled to Constantinople with the spiritual discipline of the Benedictine monasteries. This formed a new basis for justice and order in Western Europe. He extended Roman papal power to the northern nations as far as Eng- land, which became a new missionary center for the evangelization of France and Germany.

Pope Gregory's idea of a Christian empire was realized when Karl der Grosse (Charlemagne) politically unified the predominantly Ger- manic Kingdoms of Western Europe. When Pope Leo III bestowed the imperial crown on him at the Christmas mass in Rome in 800, the regal authority of Christ was seen as flowing through popes to emperors, kings and nobles, as well as bishops and priests, abbots and monks.

This unification of a "bechurched" Western Europe, however, was the beginning of the separation from Byzantine Eastern Europe. The Roman Empire and Emperor with capital at Constaninople still laid claim to European jurisdiction. From Byzantium's standpoint, Karl der Grosse was a usurper and the Pope's claims to ecclesiastical and political jurisdiction, an affront. A tenuous unity was maintained until the schism of 1054. The final rupture followed the disgraceful sack of Christian Constantinople by Western Christian crusaders in the Fourth Crusade (1204), presumably aimed at wresting the holy land from the Muslims. This tragic division left the way clear for the development of the Roman Catholic Church in Central and Western Europe as we now know it.

The Roman Catholic Church is the major church in the Central and East European nations of Poland, Lithuania, Czechoslovakia, Au- stria and Hungary; in the West European countries of Italy, Spain,

Portugal, France, Belgium and Ireland; and in the republics of Croatia and Slovenia in Yugoslavia. It also ministers to a significant number in Germany, Great Britain, the Netherlands, Romania and Switzerland. Its total baptized membership in Europe is approximately 250 million; the percentage attending mass each Sunday varies from 10 percent in some countries to as high as 80 percent in others.

One Roman Catholic country where religious practice remains high is Poland, which has received world attention since the election on October 16, 1978 of Cardinal Karol Wojtyla as Pope John Paul II. An active participant in Vatican Council II, he worked especially on *Gaudium et Spes,* the new ''Pastoral Constitution on the Church in the Modern World.'' His national church has had to move into the modern world within a communist state since 1945, but, to the surprise of many in the West, it is stronger now than it has been in decades, perhaps in centuries. The statistics comparing the church's institutional strength prior to World War II to the situation 35 years later tell part of the story:

	1937	1972
Dioceses	20	27
Parishes	5,170	6,470
Priests	11,239	18,650
Churches and Chapels	7,257	13,600
Monks and Nuns	24,000	35,550

The Catholic association *Caritas* in Poland maintains 194 institutions for the ill, handicapped and elderly; 870 Polish priests and religious served as missionaries abroad in 1975; and the only religious university remaining in the whole of Eastern Europe is the Catholic University at Lublin. More on the continued growth of the church will be found in the contemporary report from Poland found in Chapter 3.

The major institutions of the Roman Catholic Church, of course, are in Western Europe, with the Vatican, major ecclesiastical universities, the Pontifical Biblical Institute and much else centered in Rome. The societies of Austria, Spain, Portugal, France, Italy, the Federal Republic of Germany and Ireland continue to be deeply influenced by the Roman Catholic Church, that influence having increased by the dynamics released through Vatican Council II (1962-65).

The Reformation of the western church launched by Luther in Germany in 1517 (preceded by the efforts of Waldo of Lyon, founder of the Waldensian Movement, in the twelfth century, of Wycliffe in England and Hus in Czechoslovakia, and followed by those of Calvin in Geneva, Zwingli in Zurich, Knox in Scotland and many others) altered the religious face of Europe in a way that continues down to today. The boundaries separating Protestant from Catholic societies remain largely as drawn in the "Peace of Westphalia" that ended the Thirty Years War in 1648. Predominantly Lutheran societies are found in Germany and Scandinavia, with significant Lutheran churches in Estonia, Latvia, Slovakia, Austria and Hungary. Reformed or Calvinist societies predominate in Switzerland, the Netherlands and Scotland, with a significant number of Reformed churches in France, Hungary and Romania. Union Churches combining Lutheran and Reformed traditions are found in Berlin-Brandenburg and the Evangelical Church of the Czech Brethren.

A state with one of the strongest Lutheran traditions in Europe is the German Democratic Republic (East Germany), where eight regional churches are united into the Federation of Evangelical Churches. Three of these regional churches are Lutheran; the others are United Churches, deriving from both Lutheran and Reformed traditions. Here in the birthplace of the Lutheran Reformation, Wittenberg, Eisenach and Magdeburg are maintained as shrines of the Reformation. It is also the only state where a majority church of Protestant confession has directly encountered Marxism-Leninism. Though no longer a state church as in Scandinavia, the Lutheran Church remains a strong communion of approximately eight million faithful in a population of 16-17 million. Bishop Schönherr provides a fascinating interpretaton of its mission in Chapter 3.

The *Innere Mission* and *Hilfswerk* of the Lutheran churches operate 52 hospitals, 87 homes for mentally and physically handicapped people, 11 maternal and child welfare homes, 280 homes for the aged, 23 children's homes, six hospices, 328 children's day centers and 419 nursing stations in the German Democratic Republic. Clergy are educated either in the faculties of theology of the state universities in Berlin, Leipzig, Halle, Jena, Rostock or Griefswald or in seminaries maintained by the churches in Naumburg, Leipzig or Berlin. There are also six schools of church music and 50 training centers for social workers to staff the institutions referred to above. Many of these are deaconesses united ecumenically in DIAKONIA. Religious publication accounts for about 12 percent of all titles published. In 1975, 550 religious books were published in 5.2 million copies, and 30 religious periodicals totaled more than 13 million copies, in over 640 editions. This high degree of religious vitality persists in spite of an urbanized and industrialized society that is perhaps the most secularized of any in Eastern Europe, with 30 percent having no church relation.

Methodists, Baptists, United Church of Christ and other denominations important in the United States remain peripherally as Free Churches in the Orthodox-Catholic-Reformed structure of European societies. In England, its country of origin, the Methodist Church now has about 600,000 members. There are 170,000 more divided among 18 other European countries, plus a million constituents who are not full members. Baptists, more numerous, are fairly well represented in Denmark, Germany, Great Britain, Hungary, Romania and Sweden. They are the largest Protestant church in the Soviet Union. The fact that the constituency of these free churches is often much larger than their membership indicates that their worshipping congregations usually have a very high percentage of their total membership. Instead, average worship attendance sometimes exceeds the membership congregations.

The Church of England is the most significant church in Great Britain (of the Anglican tradition). Space does not allow specifying the ecumenical influence and rich synthesis of Catholic and Reformed traditions expressed through its 20,000 churches. Nor can we adequately portray the Old Catholic Church, with its most significant center in Utrecht in the Netherlands, or its branch the Polish Catholic Church, the Czechoslovak Hussite Church and other Catholic churches that do not accept the authority of the Roman papacy. Just mention of them reveals the rich variety and continuing vitality of European church life.

Variety of Church-State Relations

Understanding the history of church-state relations in Europe is essential to understanding the contemporary mission of European churches. Their ministries of peace and justice are both required and limited by their relationship to their various states.

Despite its appreciation for the peace Rome brought to the whole Mediterranean world, the earliest church drew a clear line beyond which the faithful should not carry their allegiance to the Roman empire or emperor. The Acts of the Martyrs tell many stories of Christians who refused even unto death to bear arms for the Roman Empire. Origen explained the reason in his reply to the Roman Celsus about 248 A.D.:

> We by our prayers vanquish all demons who stir up war, and lead to the violation of oaths, and disturb the peace, and in this way are much more helpful to the Kings than those who go into the field to fight for them.[5]

Early Christians shunned all forms of emperor worship and refused to give any religious allegiance to the empire as such.

Early Orthodoxy

A fundamental shift in church-state relations occurred early in the fourth century, however, when the Emperor Constantine not only legalized Christianity but began granting it many privileges. From the fourth to the eighth centuries the Roman Empire, now centered in Constantinople, moved toward becoming a "Christian Empire." The church increasingly shared the state's judicial authority and took control of much public welfare. It used imperial funds to build magnificent church buildings like the Hagia Sophia in the new capital.

Because the Byzantine Emperor now reigned over an empire that at least legally was Christian, he came to be regarded as the earthly expression of the heavenly power of Christ. The goal, as Orthodoxy now understands it, was a "symphony" between church and state. Some early emperors, however, took advantage of the church's spiritual authority to support and extend their political power. Emperors Leo III (717-741) and Constantine V (741-775), claiming absolute spiritual and temporal power, sought as both "priest and king" to make their earthly empire a replica of the Kingdom of Heaven.

This theocratic totalitarianism, sometimes called "caesaropapism," was checked in the ninth century when the rights of the emperor and those of the patriarch as head of the church were more clearly defined. The emperors were no longer in a position to impose their absolute will on the Byzantine Church. The evident danger in a "Christian society" that is an earthly empire is forgetting that God's Kingdom will only be fully realized in the eschatological future. As the church realized this, it sought to safeguard the heart of its gospel through monasticism.

With no longer a need for martyrs to mark the line of confrontation between state and church, the monks became "white" martyrs who died daily to the vain glory and luxury offered by the state. Early monastic communes also developed work disciplines that made them prosperous economic cooperatives. The monks gained vast spiritual and social influence, balancing the power of both emperor and bishop by pointing to the transcendent and eschatological dimensions of God's reign.

Orthodoxy also moved to protect the heart of its liturgy. This hadn't been necessary before Christianity became the religion of the empire, when the non-baptized were forbidden to enter the church and catechumens could not yet participate in the eucharist. However, as great sanctuaries filled with many who were superficially baptized, the heart of the liturgy was withdrawn behind an ikon wall where the laity were forbidden to enter. Monasticism and the move to safeguard the liturgy within a "Christian empire" were finally joined by the rule that a bishop presiding over the sacramental mystery in the sanctuary had to come from a monastic community.

Medieval Catholicism

Charlemagne (Karl der Grosse) was founding a West European empire just as the greatest struggle over imperial attempts at theocratic totalitarianism was taking place in the East. When a plan to unite the two empires by his marriage to the reigning Byzantine empress failed, Charlemagne began the process toward religious schism by meddling in the religious controversies of the Eastern Empire.

Beginning in the eighth century, the history of Western Europe is characterized by the struggle between Charlemagne's imperial successors and the papacy. Though neither really holy nor Roman, the Holy Roman Empire claimed not only to inherit the majesty of Rome but sometimes even the "holy" prerogative of naming popes and bishops. Otto I of Saxony, crowned Holy Roman Emperor in 962, was the first ruler to depose the pope who had crowned him. His grandson, Emperor Otto III (983-1002) chose popes as he liked. One was his chaplain and cousin, and another, his tutor.

Sometimes strong popes reciprocated. When in 1077 Emperor Henry IV sought to depose Gregory VII, he was excommunicated and his subjects released from their oaths to him. The repentant emperor was forced to stand barefoot in the snow three different days outside the castle Gregory was occupying in order to receive absolution.

When "universal" pope and "absolute" emperor cooperated, however, they gave Christian form to the ethos, loyalties, institutions and expectations of the people of Europe. Monasticism, especially in St. Benedict's rule, strongly influenced both church and society. As Friederich Heer put it in his *Intellectual History of Europe*, "Benedict's Rule was the first constitutional charter of Western Europe, ... the monks became the first Europeans."[6] The popes, especially Gregory the Great in the sixth century and Gregory VII in the eleventh century, spread and renewed this "charter" beyond the monastic enclaves throughout Europe.

The struggle between pope and emperor on the political level was over whether Roman nobles or Germanic or French kings should dominate the church. On the cultural-spiritual level the controversy centered around whether the church's leaders or a temporal ruler should have the most influence over the basis for European cultural unity. The papacy under Innocent III (1198-1216) claimed an indisputable victory over the medieval empire on this point. This was codified in the encyclical *Unam sanctum* (1302) of Boniface VIII asserting that temporal powers are subject to the spiritual authority vested in the Pope, whom only God may judge.

This high water mark of the papal claim to supremacy over civil powers came, however, just when national sentiments, especially in France and England, began to undermine the unity of Europe. The nationalism of various nations has eaten away at the fabric of European unity ever since. Today even the freest church lives in a "sovereign" state.[7]

The process of nationalism was advanced by the need of reformers for "godly princes" to protect the Reformation from the combined power of the Roman Catholic Church and the Holy Roman Empire. Though intended as only an emergency measure in a time of dangerous transformation, such dependence—especially that of Lutheran churches—led to the closest unions between state and church. While the churches gained through the Reformation, they lost when it came to the precarious balance between state and church they inherited as the result of centuries of struggle by the Orthodox Churches in the Eastern Empire and the Catholic Churches in the Western Empire.

State and National Churches

Today there are state churches in some West European countries. On the supposition that the whole nation is Christian, they depend upon the state to build their organization and educational system. State churches in their purest form are the Lutheran churches of Scandinavia, where the state maintains religious instruction for all children in the schools, supports theological faculties for the training of clergy in the state universities, and has a decisive voice in the election of bishops and the administration of the church.

The General Assembly of the Church of Sweden, for example, cannot legislate without the assent of parliament or make any decisions independent of the king's approval. All of its clergy are functionaries of the state and keep the civil register. In Norway, the Evangelical Lutheran Church is even more closely tied to the state, with no independent synod, assembly or consistory. The state appoints and maintains the bishops and ministers. The situation is much the same in Denmark, where the state is responsible for the general administration of the whole church. Fortunately the attitude of the Scandinavian governments toward these churches is fundamentally friendly and liberal.

The difference between a state and national church is not always entirely clear in history or practice. Basically a church is a national church when a large majority of the population belongs to it, and the nation state provides it certain privileges and support while allowing freedom for self-determination. The best examples are the regional Lutheran or United churches in the Federal Republic of Germany and the Reformed churches in the cantons of Switzerland. Here, church taxes collected by the government from almost all citizens support the national churches while not directly compromising their internal freedom.

Toward Free Churches

Those nations, especially in Central Europe where neither the Reformation nor Counter-Reformation was entirely successful, have

"In every village, town and city in North America the unity of Christ's church is as important locally as it is for the people of Europe continentally." Here are four churches from four points in North America that attest architecturally to the historic ties to Europe.

had to move toward toleration and freedom after the period of religious wars, the impact of the enlightenment and the emergence of liberal democracies.

The Austro-Hungarian empire, a center of the Counter-Reformation, moved slowly in this direction. The part where the Hussite Reformation originated in the fifteenth century became independent Czechoslovakia in 1920 and granted full religious liberty in its constitution at that time. An immediate result was that 1.5 million persons left the Roman Catholic Church. Many of them founded the Czechoslovak Hussite Church. Though the Roman Church in Czechoslovakia remains by far the largest, the Orthodox and Protestant churches achieved full religious autonomy.

Though the majority Roman Catholic Church retained its privileged positions in Hungary until the communist government came to power, the Hungarian state has recognized the religious autonomy and equality of rights of all churches since 1848. This was especially important for the Reformed Church in Hungary, which numbers about 2 million adherents in a population of 10.5 million.

Even in the center of the old empire, Austria, where the vast majority of the population remains Roman Catholic, full personal religious liberty was granted in 1848 and equality of rights for Lutheran and Reformed churches, in 1861. The interconfessional law of 1869 permitted a change of religion after the age of 14. Formation of new Evangelical parishes was allowed after 1875. An Evangelical theological faculty, beside the much larger Roman Catholic faculty, is maintained in the University of Vienna.

The development of free churches in pluralistic societies has been slow and achieved with great difficulty in some areas, with less difficulty in others. The Netherlands is an example of the latter. Though only members of the Reformed Church could occupy public posts until 1798, by 1848 church and state were separated, except for the subsidy provided the Reformed Church by the state. The Constitution of 1922 assured full religious liberty for all citizens and churches.

There is, of course, a difference between churches becoming free churches out of a history where they have been state or national churches, and the smaller free churches of the Methodist, Baptist and Congregational types, which always have been independent of the state. Yet even they benefit as the Lutheran and Reformed churches become free in a Europe that accepts and values freedom of conscience with its attendant pluralism. Even Scandinavia, with its continuing state churches, tolerates churches independent of the state.

Roman Catholic Concordats

The Roman Catholic Church in the nineteenth and twentieth centuries has governed its relations with sovereign nation states by means of the "concordat," a freely concluded treaty between two equally sovereign powers that legally regulates all relations between them. These concordats negotiated by the Vatican have contributed to the growth of centralized power in the Roman Church. The concordat with Napoleon's France in 1802 showed the way to later ones, which protected the church's authority to govern its own life while specifying its right to participate in the educational process of the nation. Often they have provided the church with certain national financial subsidies, based on a capitalization of the value of church properties previously secularized or nationalized in earlier centuries.

Orthodox Church-State Relations in Eastern Europe

As we have seen, a close but precariously balanced cooperation grew up between state and church in the Eastern Empire. Orthodox theology teaches that both state and church are instituted by God. They belong together though each is independent in its own field, and act "symphonically" in fields that require common action. A favorite metaphor is that state and church are related to one another as body and soul are.

This ideal, always difficult to realize, became even more so after the empire fell to the Ottoman Muslims. One consequence was that the church became the last refuge of national cultural life, as in Bulgaria. As church and nation under Muslim rule were bound more closely together, there was an unprecedented increase in religious nationalism. This affects Orthodox churches even today.

The freedom the Orthodox Church theologically claimed has been overridden by the state under other circumstances, too, as in Czarist Russia when the Princes of Moscow conceived themselves as the Czars (Caesars) of a Third Rome. The Russian church had been more independent when it represented the church universal through loyalty to the ecumenical patriarch in Constantinople, but Constantinople's fall to the Muslims in 1453 ended that. Prince Ivan III's marriage to the niece of the last Byzantine emperor in 1472 provided the basis for his descendants' theocratic dream of inheriting the power of Constantinople as the Third Rome. In 1569 Moscow's Metropolitan Philip of the Orthodox Church paid with his life for seeking to use the spiritual authority of the church to limit the growing despotism of Ivan the Terrible, who had become the first Czar "by God's mercy" 12 years earlier.

In 1721, Czar Peter the Great entirely abolished the patriarchate, which had made the Russian church self-governing since 1589. He appointed a lay procurator who became the de facto administrative head of the Holy Synod. The Russian church for the next 200 years became bureaucratically what it was named in imperial terminology, "the Department of the Orthodox Confession." Czar Peter's absolutism denied the church any right to be the conscience of the state; the Russian Orthodox Church became in fact a state church whose Holy Synod had to recognize the emperor as its "high judge." It could promulgate its decisions only by the authority granted by the emperor. The similarity with the Lutheran state churches is clear. The Lutheran pattern may have directly influenced this western-oriented Czar.

The effect of the communist revolution on Russian church-state relations in what is now the Soviet Union is highly paradoxical. On the one hand, as early as the decree of January 1918, church and state were separated, and the church under its own patriarch was freer than at any time since Ivan the Terrible to govern its own affairs. On the other hand, the ruling communist party has shown itself so ideologically hostile to the church that state power has been used to try to shut the church up in its own sanctuaries, cut it off from any social influence and, during the period of Stalinist tyranny in the 1930s, even destroy the church as such. Religious liberty, wherein church and state are separated by the constitution, too often has become religious persecution at worst, or severe limitation at best. Nevertheless, the Russian Orthodox Church has reconstituted its patriarchate, maintained the integrity of its episcopacy and priesthood, reconstituted a small number of its seminaries and academies, entered strongly into the ecumenical movement and maintained one of the most beautiful and movingly devotional liturgical traditions in the world. It is not yet clear which side of this tragic paradox will become the dominant reality in the future, but the spiritual freedom and vitality of the church within the severe limitations set by the Soviet state are clearly established after more than six decades.

Roots of North American
Religious Problems and Possibilities

The proliferation of churches in North America is our inheritance from this whole complex European history. The patterns of migration from Europe left not only their ethnic/national but their churchly imprint on our societies. For example, the fact that much of our southwest was first settled by Spanish people explains the heavy concentration of Roman Catholic Christians in that region. Scandinavian and German immigrants found Wisconsin, Minnesota and the Dakotas similar to the climate for agriculture they left, which helps us understand the concentration of Lutherans in that area. The early English settlements on the eastern seaboard explain the number of Congregational and Episcopal churches there and later in Canada. The "free" character of the Methodist and Baptist churches, in the sense of not being organically tied to one nationality, undoubtedly led to their following the frontier and becoming the most comprehensively national of any of our US Protestant churches.

However, the internal mobility of ethnic groups, especially in the twentieth century, means that this churchly mapping of North America according to European origins no longer makes as much sense as it did. We have never had the degree of regional religious homogeneity some European nations still have, but there was a time when we had clearer majority traditions in certain regions of our country. The religious pluralism that first evidenced itself in our great metropolitan centers now is found in every locality across our country.

The Importance of Ecumenicity

This means that in every village, town and city in North America the unity of Christ's church is as important locally as it is for the people of Europe continentally. It is almost as though Europe has played "fruit basket upset" to set itself down with all of its diversity in most of our communities. To understand these various European traditions and appreciate their continuing vitality is to recognize the richness that ecumenical "conciliar fellowship" offers all of our churches.

The fact that the present major effort toward organic union of nine churches in North America, the Consultation on Church Union (COCU), describes the intended church as "truly catholic, truly evangelical, and truly reformed" does indicate, however—by the

27

adjective omitted—that "orthodox" Christians are not yet strongly represented among us. There are, of course, understandable reasons why "orthodoxy" is not crucial to COCU, but it is becoming ever more clear that Eastern Orthodoxy must become a more important part of our ecumenical experience in North America. Clearly, they are in the best position to help us understand what our Christian response to East European communist and Middle Eastern Muslim societies should be. We have much to learn from the wisdom of their long historical experience and the challenges they face today.

The Danger of Civil Religion

The need to deal with communist and Muslim relations brings us finally to the recognition of the role of civil religion in North American societies. How do our Christian people react to Iran, Cuba or the Soviet Union? The fact that no one church could be a state or national church for the American or Canadian people has led to the development in the United States, and to a lesser extent in Canada, of a "civil religion" quite separate from the churches. Professor Sydney Mead, in his essay on "The Nation With the Soul of a Church," wrote that "in a very real sense the nation for many Americans came to occupy the place in their lives that traditionally has been occupied by the church."[8]

Sometimes our civil religion has been profound, as expressed in Abraham Lincoln's second inaugural address or Martin Luther King, Jr.'s definition of his "dream" for America before 250,000 people at the Lincoln Memorial in 1963. But civil religion also has been misused ideologically to protect the national and economic interests of the dominant white race, middle class and masculine gender in our societies. It is at these points of conflict in the struggles for peace and justice that we North American Christians must learn to distance ourselves from our civil religion in the way that European Christians have learned to criticize the ideological dimensions in their state and national churches. Perhaps together we can Christianly transcend our various social and national structures to discern through the gospel, ecumenically understood, how truly to witness to Jesus Christ and the peace with justice he offers.

Discussion Questions for Chapter 1

1. *Do the people of the congregations with whom you are best acquainted know as much about the churches of Eastern Europe as about those in Western Europe or Africa? If not, why not? Do you think it important that we know these churches better?*
2. *Did you realize that the churches in "communist" East Europe are, on the whole, stronger worshiping communities than those in "free" Western Europe? How do you explain this surprising phenomenon?*
3. *The North American pattern of separation of church and state is closer to the present pattern of Eastern Europe than to most of Western Europe, yet there are great differences. How are North American churches similar to and different from the state and national churches of Western Europe? How are they similar to and different from the "free" churches of Eastern Europe?*
4. *Why does "civil religion" play a more important role in the United States, and perhaps also in Canada, than in Europe? What else could unify the value commitments of North Americans? Would we be better off with a "national church" like Poland or Romania, though church and state are legally separated? What values and dangers to the mission of the churches are found in our pattern of many churches plus civil religion?*

2. The Permanence and Permeability of Walls in Europe

Theological Perspective

"Walls" constitute a part of the enduring image of Europe in most North American minds: ancient walled cities, fenced estates and carefully guarded border crossings. This image of life in a Europe divided, restricted and protected by walls contrasts strongly with the openness of American existence. No military or tariff barriers mark the frontiers of the states and provinces making up the United States and Canada. The borders that separate Canada and Mexico from the United States are remarkably open by many European standards.

Winston Churchill's rhetoric in 1946 of an "iron curtain" dividing Eastern and Western Europe after World War II reinforced this image of "European walls" for North Americans. In 1961 the image became reality when the "Berlin wall" literally cut a great city, and indeed a whole nation, in two. Many of the 2.2 million residents of West Berlin were the children, parents and grandparents of some of the 1.1 million people in East Berlin, from whom they were separated by concrete and barbed wire. For more than a decade the only telephone communication was by long distance via Frankfurt, often requiring a wait of up to 24 hours. Only in such rare circumstances as the grave illness of a parent could families be together even for a brief time. With so many tragic stories added to the drama of the "wall" depicted in our mass media, the "iron curtain" image continues in North American parlance long after much of its reality has eroded.

The founding of a truly conciliar community, the World Council of Churches, is seen here at the gathering of the First Assembly, Amsterdam, 1948.

The erosion of the walls that political, economic and ethnic conflicts have erected is partly the result of the remarkable resilience of Christian community in Europe. Though existing in great variety because of the histories that separate European peoples, the churches transcend those histories through their allegiance to a universal gospel. The teaching and preaching of all include such powerful texts as, "Jesus Christ is our peace, who has made us both one, and has *broken down the dividing wall of hostility*" (Ephesians 2:14).

The good news of Christian proclamation includes Christ's victory over the hostilities dividing human beings. This does not mean that a Christian's perception of quite real walls is somehow dulled. If anything, Christian sensitivity to the human tragedy created by such walls is heightened by the gospel. Rather, it means that the life of faith and the community of the faithful are found on both sides of every wall. The Christians thus experience every political, economic or ethnic wall as provisional and penetrable. No wall reaches to heaven nor penetrates the heart, for heaven belongs to Christ who guards faithful hearts.

It is characteristic of Christians to move through walls regularly, whether by prayer, letter, gift or travel. Those whose tragic business it is to build and tend walls are met with the open assurance that keeping walls is not enough to fill any person's life. There is no great surprise when even the keepers of walls respond with humanity. Representatives of Christ's churches should make no great adventure out of crossing the world's walls, just because they are still there. Nor should Christians take themselves too seriously for crossing the walls Christ already has overcome. The penetration of walls must increasingly become a commonplace for Christians.

The Emergence of Conciliar Christianity

Nothing has so enhanced the mission of contemporary Christianity as the development of a conciliar community that allows churches to transcend many national boundaries. Understandably, North American Anglicans and Protestants think first of the founding of the World Council of Churches in Amsterdam in 1948, though actually this event was preceded in 1947 by European deaconesses organizing the World Federation of Deaconess Associations called Diakonia. European Protestants and Orthodox Christians remember the founding of the Conference of European Churches in Nyborg, Denmark in 1959.

Nothing so dramatically illustrates the point, however, as the convening of the Roman Catholic Church's Vatican Council II in October, 1962. Pope John XXIII's first announcement on January 25, 1959 of his plan to convene the 21st Ecumenical Council of his Church had almost coincided with the first full assembly of the Conference of European Churches, January 6-9.

But a far more fateful coincidence of events attended the opening of Vatican Council II on October 11, 1962, at the precise time the "iron curtain" dividing east and west threatened to explode in a nuclear apocalypse that could destroy most of European and North American civilization. Only a year after the ill-fated US invasion of Cuba, US reconnaissance had identified the preparation in Cuba of 42 launching sites for nuclear missiles aimed at the United States. Steaming toward Cuba were 25 Soviet ships, some laden with the dreaded missiles. With an American fleet including eight aircraft carriers and 68 air squadrons set on a course to intercept them, the whole northern hemisphere hovered at the edge of the nuclear abyss.

The words of assurance with which Pope John had opened the Council ten days before—"Providence is leading the world to a new order of human relationships. Experience has let men test the absolute insufficiency of weapons' brute force"[1]—appeared to be denied in the prospect of thermonuclear war. For a few dark hours it looked as though Billy Graham's announcement in Buenos Aires of the imminent "end of the world" was proving more prophetic. There was even thought of suspending the Council so that the 2,240 bishops could return to their dioceses before the unthinkable happened.

What did happen, however, was the intervention of Pope John that helped turn both the Soviet and American governments from confrontation to negotiation. The Vatican's frequent denunciation of communism gave way to a public statement recognizing the possibility of a communist commitment to peace. For the first time, *Tass*, a Soviet newspaper, reported a religious event, emphasizing the affirmation of the Council's October 20th "Message to the World": "There does not exist a man who does not detest war and tend toward peace with ardent desire." When papal messengers called at Soviet and American embassies in Rome for "discussion at all levels and in all times as a rule of wisdom and prudence that will call down the blessing of heaven on earth," both governments responded. The world was temporarily spared nuclear holocaust. The importance of the church's role in averting this crisis led to John XXIII's decision to begin his most important encyclical, *Pacem in Terris*.

MUST WALLS DIVIDE?

This dramatic event focuses the continuous, if less dramatic, conciliar mission of the churches. The Conference of European Churches began in 1959 with representatives from only 45 churches. By the time it saluted its twentieth anniversary during its Eighth Assembly in Crete, October 18-25, 1979, 112 member churches gathered for the conference. At first there was only limited representation of the Orthodox Churches of Eastern Europe, but now virtually all the Orthodox Churches of Europe join almost all the Protestant and Anglican churches of Europe in the Council's increasingly active life. The small group of "observers" sent to the Fourth Assembly in 1964 by the Roman Catholic Church was the first step to a growing cooperation with the Roman Catholic Church. More of the work of this Council will be reported in Chapter 4.

Because most of our churches are members of the World Council of Churches, its work is better known to us. Made all the more urgent by World War II, which interrupted its ten years of preparation, the WCC was officially established in Amsterdam in 1948 with a membership drawn from 147 churches around the world, primarily Western Europe and North America. By its Fifth Assembly in Nairobi, Kenya in 1975, it had grown to 286 member churches representing more than 90 countries of every race, economic class and political system. With its headquarters in Geneva, Switzerland, and much of its early leadership coming from European churches, for all practical purposes it had served as a European Council of Churches during the first decade of its existence. As the WCC became ever more fully a *world* council, however, the unique mission of the European churches required the increased missional activity of the Conference of European Churches.

The Christian Peace Conference, the semi-official ecumenical organization based in Eastern Europe that emerged during the 1950s, is much less known among North Americans. It emerged when 200 representatives of the Czech churches came together at the initiative of the Ecumenical Council of Churches in Czechoslovakia to discuss "The Struggle against Thermonuclear Weapons as a Task of the Church," at the height of the cold war in 1957. Quickly discerning that effective efforts against the threatening nuclear holocaust required international structures, they called together the first Christian Peace Conference, June 1-4, 1958 in Prague. Only 40 representatives from churches in Bulgaria, Romania, Hungary, the Soviet Union, Czechoslovakia, the German Democratic Republic and the Federal Republic of Germany came. From this meager beginning, where

34

almost all representatives were from Eastern Europe, they projected the first All-Christian Peace Assembly, which brought to Prague, June 13-18, 1961, 600 participants from 42 countries.

Not least of the ecumenical services of the Christian Peace Conference was bringing the Russian Orthodox and other eastern churches from 30 years of isolation into ecumenical community and dialogue. This prepared the way for their entrance into the World Council of Churches in 1961. We will discuss some of the continuing work of the CPC in Chapter 4.

In addition to these ecumenical structures, international bodies uniting families of churches in common mission continued and expanded their work after World War II. Chief among these are the Anglican Consultative Council, the Baptist World Alliance (which includes the European Baptist Federation), the Lutheran World Federation, the World Alliance of Reformed Churches and the World Methodist Council. The Reformed and Lutheran structures share the Ecumenical Center in Geneva, Switzerland, with the World Council of Churches and the Conference of European Churches. The Anglican Council is based in England, while the Baptist and Methodist structures have their headquarters in the United States.

European Political and Economic Blocs

During the last 30 years European churches have had to struggle against the background of solidifying political and economic division to realize their unity in Christ. Europe today is almost entirely divided into two political and economic blocs. The North American press tends to feature the military aspects of these blocs: the North Atlantic Treaty Organization (NATO) and the Warsaw Pact Powers. Until a war breaks out, however, it is probably the economic structures that have the most effect on the well-being of the people. Because political and economic factors cannot be disjoined, we must try to understand the two forms of political economy that characterize the two blocs.

Western Europe began to organize itself into one cooperative economic unit when six nations—Belgium, the Federal Republic of Germany, France, Italy, Luxembourg and the Netherlands—formed the European Coal and Steel Community (ECSE) in 1952, and the European Economic Community (EEC) in 1958. In 1973, Denmark, Ireland and the United Kingdom were added. Greece is scheduled to join in 1981, and Spain and Portugal, in 1983. Thus, all of Western Europe except Finland, Norway and Sweden soon will be members.

In 1967, ECSE and EEC, along with the European Atomic Energy Community, joined in a single structure called "The European Community," with a staff of 7,000 headquartered in Brussels. The main decision-making body has been the Council of Ministers, composed of Ministers from each member state. The first direct elections of the European Parliament, however, were held June 7-10, 1979. In time this may limit some national sovereignty as the parliament pushes for a greater voice in policy decisions.

Some sovereignty over economic planning already has been given up. A Common Agricultural Policy, for instance, has been developed to guarantee food supplies for the 260 million people of the European Community and stable, reasonable prices for its farmers. During the latter half of the seventies, the Community also has moved slowly toward a common energy policy and to reduce the dependency on oil imports. This is even more crucial for Western Europe, with much less domestic gas and oil, than it is for North America.

The western countries of the European Community that ruled over many colonial territories until the last half of the twentieth century have developed a common policy toward these new nations as well. In 1975 the European Community entered into the Lome Agreement with more than 50 former colonies in Africa, the Caribbean and the Pacific. This provided duty-free entry into the EC of some products and financial and technical assistance to these developing nations. Negotiations for a Lome II Agreement to go into force in 1980 were completed in 1979.

North America, and especially the United States, maintains close relations with the European Community. Delegations from the US Congress and the European Parliament, as well as high level US and EC administrative officials, meet twice each year to deal with such subjects as energy, trade and relations with the Third World. In 1978, the US exported $32.4 billion to the European Community and imported $29.4 billion from it. It is no wonder that former US Secretary of State Cyrus Vance said in a 1978 speech on the "The US-European Partnership":

> We have established a pattern of closer consultation on economic and security matters than at any point in recent history. European integration is proceeding, confirming our belief that a strong Europe is good for a strong America.[2]

Unfortunately, he meant Western Europe, not Europe as a whole.

Similar statements come from representatives of the Soviet Union concerning the economic integration of the East European countries. The Council for Mutual Economic Assistance (Comecon or CMEA), now includes as members Bulgaria, Czechoslovakia, the German Democratic Republic, Hungary, Mongolia, Poland, Romania, the Soviet Union, Cuba and Vietnam. On the occasion of its thirtieth anniversary, in Moscow, June 26-28, 1979, Premier Alexei Kosygin of the Soviet Union celebrated the "principles of socialist internationalism" with the observation that:

> Within a short historical period the CMEA countries have turned themselves into a monolithic group of states with a progressive economic structure.[3]

There is a fundamental difference, however, between the Soviet Union's relationship to the CMEA countries, and the USA's to EC countries. The CMEA countries are economically more dependent on the Soviet Union than the EC countries on the USA. No one of the East European countries, or all of them together, can approach the economic strength of the Soviet Union, while the economic strength of Western Europe and the USA is much more equal. Eastern European countries depend on the Soviet Union for most of their energy resources, as between 1976 and 1980 when the USSR supplied CMEA countries with 370 million tons of crude oil, 46 million tons of petroleum products, and 80 billion cubic meters of gas. United Nations statistics indicate that in 1978 all of Eastern Europe produced only 223,836,000 metric tons of hard coal compared to the Soviet Union's production of 723,996,000 tons; the same year the Soviet Union produced 150,996,000 metric tons of steel, while all of Eastern Europe produced only 47,856,000 tons.

No East European country except Czechoslovakia was highly industrialized before World War II; even the eastern part of Germany had been largely agricultural. None had the capital and technical assistance of Marshall Plan aid from the USA to repair and rebuild after the war as did Western Europe, though some would gladly have received it if the Soviet Union had allowed it. In contrast to Western Germany, Eastern Germany had to pay reparations to the Soviet Union immediately after the war. As a result, recovery from the devastation of World War II proceeded more slowly for all of Eastern Europe than in Western Europe.

The economic strength of these two European blocs remains quite unequal. A Special Report of the US Department of State in December, 1978 comparing East-West economic strength as of 1977 gave the gross national product (GNP) in billions of dollars as 2,036 for Western Europe, 350 for Eastern Europe and 932 for the Soviet Union. With the 388 million population of Western Europe roughly equivalent to the 110 million in Eastern Europe plus 259 million in the Soviet Union, it is clear that the per capita GNP is significantly lower in the East: $5,251 for Western Europe, $3,176 for Eastern Europe and $3,600 for the Soviet Union. In 1977 the per capita GNP for the USA was $8,704 and for Canada $8,447.

> For other significant comparisons, it was $283 for the People's Republic of China and estimated at $524 for the rest of the Third World.

The economic growth rates of Eastern European countries, however, exceeded those of Western Europe. Statistics in the *1980 Britannica Book of the Year* indicate that the economies of Western Europe grew at a rate of about 4 percent between 1965 and 1975. In contrast, the economic growth rate in the East in the same period was roughly 8 percent. A decline in the East's economic growth rate, however, has moved the figures so that there is little difference at this point: Western Europe's GNP was growing at just over 3 percent in 1979, with Eastern Europe's at 4 percent.

The major structural difference between these political economies is in the planning and capital allocation process. Planning in the eastern countries is highly centralized. National ministries for the various industries develop national plans, which follow policy decisions of the central organs of the ruling Communist Parties. Bloc coordination is through CMEA. In the western countries the planning and capital allocation process is shared by the major private corporations and banks, and the governmental ministries. Bloc coordination is through the EC. In Western Europe where democratic socialist or more traditional or middle-class political parties organize the governments, policy decisions are made in more democratically elected parliaments.

Economic Organization and Human Need

The comparative efficacy of these two systems in meeting the basic needs of their people and contributing to their overall well-being is one of the most disputed issues in our contemporary world. Objective criteria may be brought to this discussion, however, since the Club of Rome called for the development of a "quality of life index" to be used in conjunction with the indicator of per capita GNP. Because money measures in themselves say nothing about the well-being of persons, the Overseas Development Council, a private group in the USA chaired by President Theodore M. Hesburgh of the University of Notre Dame, developed a "Physical Quality of Life Index" (PQLI) to measure how well the basic human needs of a people are met. This index consolidates average life expectancy, infant mortality and literacy rate in a composite index of 1-100, giving equal weight to each of the three indicators. A PQLI provides objective data for comparing how well a given country satisfies the nutritional, medical and educational needs of its people.[4]

The Overseas Development Council uses its index principally to assess the quality of development in Third World countries. There is, of course, some correlation between per capita GNP and the Physical Quality of Life Index, because resources must be developed before food, education and medical care can be provided. But there is not as close a correlation as some might expect. For instance, in 1976 Iran had a per capital GNP of $1,930, but a PQLI of 52, while Sri Lanka had a PQLI of 82 with a per capita GNP of only $200.

What do the statistics developed by the Overseas Development Council tell us about Eastern and Western Europe? Primarily, that these two blocs do about equally well in meeting the basic needs of their people, as the following table using 1976 data shows:

	Eastern Europe		
COUNTRY	POPULATION (MILLIONS)	PER CAPITA GNP ($)	PQLI
Romania	21.9	1,450	91
Hungary	10.7	2,280	90
Bulgaria	8.8	2,310	92
Soviet Union	261.0	2,760	91
Poland	35.1	2,860	92
Czechoslovakia	15.2	3,840	93
GDR	16.7	4,220	94

Western Europe

COUNTRY	POPULATION (MILLIONS)	PER CAPITA GNP ($)	PQLI
Ireland	3.2	2,560	92
Greece	9.3	2,590	89
Spain	36.8	2,920	92
Netherlands	13.9	6,200	96
France	53.4	6,550	95
Belgium	9.9	6,780	93
FRG	61.3	7,380	94

It is interesting to note, for instance, that Romania with a low per capita GNP of $1,450 still keeps its PQLI at 91, indicating a good use of limited resources. The most direct comparison is between the two Germanys, each having the largest GNP in its respective bloc and exactly the same PQLI of 94. While the Eastern countries keep their PQLI roughly equivalent to the Western countries, they apportion only about half the production of the West. Using 1976 data, the PQLI rating for both Canada and the USA is 95. The top PQLI rating is Sweden's, at 97.

Perhaps the most revealing statistic developed by the Overseas Development Council, the Physical Quality of Life Index is given for only a few European nation-states, allowing comparison of only three from the East with three from the West. What the following table shows is the per capita GNP growth rate in relation to the increase in the PQLI between 1960 and 1970.[5]

COUNTRY	GNP GROWTH RATE 1960–1970	PQLI 1960	PQLI 1970
Hungary	5.4%	87.1	90.1
Poland	5.2	85.1	91.6
Romania	7.1	77.1	86.6
Greece	6.6	84.3	88.4
Belgium	4.0	90.3	92.8
France	4.6	91.2	94.9

Note that Greece and Romania had roughly comparable growth rates, but Romania's PQLI advanced by 9.5 points while Greece improved by only 4.1 points. While Poland and France also had roughly comparable per capita GNP growth, Poland advanced its PQLI 6.5 as compared to France's 3.7. Hungary and Belgium's increase in the PQLI is more directly in ratio to their GNP growth rates.

These statistics suggest that though Eastern Europe began from a poorer position, it has deployed its growing economic resources in a way that successfully meets the basic needs of its people. It is, of course, also true, as portrayed by western mass media, that many consumer goods, especially luxurious consumer items such as private automobiles, are in short supply in Eastern Europe. The Soviet Union also must import food, especially grain, to provide for its growing population as large a diet of meat as they plan. The short growing season and mode of organizing agriculture combine to keep the USSR from becoming self-sufficient in food production.

It is interesting that Poland, the East European state with the second largest population and agricultural production, has not followed the Soviet Union's pattern in collectivizing agriculture. Of Poland's agricultural land, 83 percent is privately owned, making 40 percent of the population private land owners. The church in Poland, as in the German Democratic Republic, also remains a rather large land owner, claiming a small acreage in almost every town and rural parish.

The less developed East European states remain somewhat dependent on the West for the most sophisticated technology and machinery. Their imports from western industrial countries exceeded exports by nearly $10 billion in 1978 and about $7 billion in 1977. The total CMEA debt to western banks was reported as approximately $53 billion in 1978, and $60 billion near the end of 1979.[6] The increase in the cost of consumer goods in order to meet payments on this growing external debt has caused severe social tensions in some Eastern countries, notably Poland.

The Burden of the Arms Race

Growth in economic well-being, however, is severely hampered by the burden of armaments created to buttress the walls still dividing the two blocs. Ruth Leger Sivard has pointed out that the world now has, in pounds per person, more explosive power than food, while eight million children die annually from hunger and illnesses related to malnutrition.[7] Most of this explosive power has been produced to fortify and perhaps violate the wall that separates one European political economic bloc from the other.

In 1976, world military expenditures totaled $356 billion or about $1 billion per day. NATO spent $150.6 billion of that, with $91 billion spent by the USA and $3.6 billion, by Canada. The Warsaw Pact spent $112.9 billion, with the Soviet Union's share, $103 billion.[8] These figures reveal that almost 75 percent of the world's military expenditures relate to the fissure running down the middle of Europe.

Even worse is the flow of weapons this monstrous arms race sends into the developing Third World nations: Sivard reports $50.3 billion worth from the USA from 1955 to 1977, $15 billion from other NATO powers (with Canada's share only $695 million), $21 billion from the Soviet Union and $2.1 billion from other Warsaw Pact nations. These weapons helped fuel 114 armed conflicts in the recipient Third World nations between 1955 and early 1979.[9] What a record misuse of resources to obstruct the genuine human development of these societies!

The cost of the arms race within Europe itself is borne far more heavily in the East than in the West, considering the disparity in average per capita GNP. Again using Sivard's statistics, military expenditure per capita in 1976 in NATO Europe was $175, while it was $311 in the Warsaw Pact countries. A direct comparison of the USA and USSR shows $423 per capita for the USA in 1976 and $401 for the Soviet Union. Canada was at $158 per capita (less than most of NATO, but more than any Warsaw Pact country except the German Democratic Republic at $174).

The arms race also reduces the amount of economic aid industrialized countries are able and willing to provide developing nations. While NATO Europe was spending $56 billion in 1976 on its military, it provided only $6.1 billion in economic aid. The proportions of the US budget are even worse. In 1976, the USA spent $91 billion for its military but provided only $4.3 billion in economic aid. The statistics for Eastern Europe, as far as they are known, are worse: $112.9 billion spent on their military, while they provided only $480 million in foreign economic aid.[10] Whether completely accurate or not, these statistics make it clear that vast resources being used to stockpile weapons along a wall in Europe might instead be providing sustenance, health and literacy to those subjugated and economically exploited by many European nations in previous centuries.

Christian-Marxist Relations

Is it any wonder that as the European church strengthened its unity—despite and perhaps even because of the wall dividing Europe—it moved not only to penetrate and destroy that wall but to resist any ideological extension of it that threatened their life or their understanding of the gospel? Given the national and folk character of European churches, how difficult it has been to prevent such a division within and between the churches. To the degree that they have not permitted walls to be erected, the churches have experienced a marvelous victory of God's grace in the midst of human conflict.

North American Christians may understand the difficulty when they remember the leadership in both church and state of John Foster Dulles, who had taken an active part in the Oxford Conference on Church, Community and State in 1937. As an international lawyer and churchman, Dulles valued the universal character of the church with its vision of world community as the only adequate antidote for the rampant nationalisms and growing international violence of the twentieth century. For a number of years he was aligned with American pacifists and noninterventionists in the effort to avert World War II and keep the United States out of that conflict. From late 1940 on, he chaired the Federal Council of Churches' Committee on a Just and Durable Peace. The key conviction he carried from the Oxford Conference was that the Church should enunciate moral principles as a basis for political action and support those political programs that foster Christian ideals.

By 1948, however, the European wall had projected itself into Dulles' Christian perspective so strongly that he declared in his address to the first assembly of the World Council of Churches entitled "Christian Responsibility in our *Divided* World":

> ... Christian citizens could feel that to extend *free* societies was a great long-range effort to which they could worthily dedicate themselves and seek to dedicate their nations.... Those engaged in that effort could feel that they were making the world more nearly one where God's will would be done.[11]

43

He now saw the church's moral principles as supporting a politics of the "free world" in a cold war against the "atheistic" politics of nation-states governed by communist parties. By the time he was US Secretary of State (1952-59), Dulles no longer understood the role of the ecumenical church as creating a universal community and common world ethos, but rather to inspire and support the West in its struggle against communism.

Mr. Dulles was challenged in the 1948 World Council Assembly by Professor Josef L. Hromadka, who had left the faculty of Princeton Theological Seminary in 1947, where he had come as a refugee almost ten years before, to return to Prague as Dean of the Comenius Theological Faculty. Dulles and Hromadka had worked together on the Federal Council of Churches' Commission on a Just and Durable Peace in 1941. Now Professor Hromadka reminded his old colleague that western self-righteousness should not disguise the ideological link between middle-class thinking and the western perspective he was articulating. Serving on the Executive Committee of the World Council of Churches from 1948 to 1968, Hromadka often pointed to what he considered the World Council's one-sided orientation to western social perspectives during that early period of its life.[12] He helped found the eastern-based Christian Peace Conference to broaden the base of ecumenicity by including more Christians from within socialist systems, and to focus the ecumenical movement more directly on peace and justice.

While the cold war was peaking in the late 1950s something totally different was being prepared through many quiet dialogues in Europe. Among these quiet, fermenting processes was the Christian-Marxist seminar that Professor Milan Machovec founded in the late 1950s and directed until 1968 in Charles University in Prague. This creative Marxist philosopher was responding to the dialogical openness of Professor Hromadka and some of his younger colleagues to Marxist concerns for justice and alienated persons in industrial societies with a similar openness to Christian faith and ethics in our contemporary world.[13]

The quiet dialogue of Machovec, Hromadka and others—barely tolerated by a conservative communist party hierarchy—burst into public view in 1968 in a Czechoslovakia led by Alexander Dubcek. My wife and I were present on April 29, 1968 for the first public Christian-Marxist dialogue in Prague when 4,000 persons crowded into a room designed for 700. They remained from 7:30 p.m. until past midnight to hear answers to the questions they posed to the dozen Marxists and Christians on the platform, under Machovec's chairmanship.

What now was publicly possible in Eastern Europe also came to prominence in the West. Both the World Council of Churches in Geneva and the Vatican in Rome sponsored Christian-Marxist dialogues in 1968. These were preceded four years earlier by groundbreaking events led by Professor Roger Garaudy in France, where the Communist Party's "Commission for Anti-Religious Studies" renamed itself the "Center for Marxist Studies and Research." Protestant theologians were invited to discuss "Humanistic or Christian Meanings of the Reformation" on the 400th anniversary of Calvin's death. The Communist Party of France was host to representatives of both the Protestant and Roman Catholic Churches in Lyon on February 20-21, 1964 at a discussion on "Materialism and Transcendence."

By 1964 the Paulus Gesellschaft (Society of St. Paul) of West Germany and Austria (founded in 1956 by Dr. Erich Kellner, a Roman Catholic priest and theologian) was convinced that dialogue with Marxists was now required. That year a symposium in Munich discussed "Man: Spirit and Matter," with one Marxist participant, Professor Ernst Bloch of the University of Tübingen in West Germany. Also in 1964, the Polish Marxist philosopher and member of the Communist Party's Central Committee, Professor Adam Schaff, was at their conference in Cologne to discuss "Christianity and Marxism Today." By the time their first international congress on "Christian and Marxist Future" was held in Salzburg, April 29–May 2, 1965, there were Marxists from France, Italy, Bulgaria, Hungary and Yugoslavia among the 250 participants. At their 1966 conference on "Christian Humanity and Marxist Humanism" at Herren Chiemsee, West Germany, the number of East European Christians and Marxists had so increased that the press and media sensationalized the news that Christians and Marxists could talk creatively with each other.

The climactic dialogue in this series was co-sponsored by the Czechoslovak Academy of Sciences at Marianske Lazny (Marienbad), CSSR. The theme was "Creativity and Freedom," and it was the first time such a conference met in Eastern Europe. It attracted the largest number of Marxists ever to participate in a dialogue with Christians. Both sides discovered that they could go beyond stereotypes to recognize a common concern for justice and the fulfill-ment of human beings in society.

The lesson learned through these dialogues was brought home to North Americans by Professor Roger Garaudy in his book, *From Anathema to Dialogue,* published in English in 1966:

> We have come to the tragic and exalting moment in the history of mankind when the human epic which began a million years ago can crumble. If the human race survives, the reason for its survival will not be the simple force of inertia of biological evolution. The race will survive because of human choice.... Hundreds of millions of men find in religious beliefs the mean-ing of life and death, and the very meaning of the history of our race, while other hundreds of millions find that Communism gives a face to the hopes of the earth and a meaning to our history. Thus it is an incontestable fact of our age that the future of man cannot be constructed either against religious believers or without them. Neither can it be constructed against the Communists or without them.[14]

With this recognition, the irony of Christians believing that social walls can be made of iron in a world where Christ overcomes walls is clear. Perhaps nationalists, colonialists, racists and assorted ideo-logues may believe that, but Christians who know and express the social meaning of their faith straightforwardly cannot. When in their right mind, they discover that many Marxists also do not believe in the walls that block human dialogue and relationships.

This dialogue does not necessarily indicate naivete on the part of Christians. They know the walls have not disappeared. The invasion of Czechoslovakia by the Soviet Union and other Warsaw Pact nations, in fact, brought the dialogue of the sixties to a close. Profes-sor Machovec was permanently shut out of his teaching position in Charles University, and Professor Schaff lost not only his position at the University of Warsaw but also his place on the Polish Central Committee because of his courageous criticism of the Czechoslova-kia invasion. For the same reason even Professor Garaudy was removed in February 1970 from his position in the Politburo and Central Committee of the French Communist Party, which he had held 14 and 24 years respectively. On the other side, the use of ideological anti-communism to justify excessive arms expenditure in the West is just as bad.

Catholic prelates from throughout the world assembled here in the nave of St. Peter's Basilica for the formal close of the first session of the Second Vatican Council.

It must be remembered that there are Marxists who at no little risk have sought to provide an interpretation of Marxism that advances the human fulfillment of everyone. Some have turned dialogically toward Christians, where they may have met the open minds and hearts one would expect. In the 1960s this was largely a European effort, but at this time we who are members of churches in the USA are responsible for Christian witness in one of the two most powerful states on earth. Increasingly in the eighties we must find our way into this dialogue to remove the ideological constraints now limiting the mission of peace and justice in so many of our churches. As we do, we shall find that this Christian-Marxist dialogue has taken a new form in the liberation struggles and theology of many of our sisters and brothers in Latin America. They, too, call for our informed and committed response.

Penetrating American Ideological Walls

It is startling for many North Americans, particularly citizens of the United States, to discover that "socialism" is a good word in many West European contexts and that the works of Karl Marx are studied in many West European universities. The degree of surprise is the measure of the misunderstanding in North American minds about this nineteenth-century philosopher whose passion for justice continues to inspire political struggle and economic reform around our world.

During his lifetime, Karl Marx thought the epoch was at hand when the vast multitudes of workers in Western Europe could break through the social structures of the developing capitalism that kept them from becoming creatively free. His historical analysis and expectation proved at least partially wrong; those he inspired in the late nineteenth and early twentieth centuries could only stimulate revolutions in pre- or little-industrialized societies in order to centralize planning and speed up the process of industrialization. This often was accomplished, especially during the Stalinist period, at the enormous personal and social cost of a Gulag Archipelago. Though compressed into a shorter period and thus, more terrible, such oppression was not unlike the exploitation of men, women and children in mine and factory—to say nothing of outright slavery—which accompanied early industrialization in Europe and North America.

It remains to be seen whether socialist societies under communist party leadership can become the kind of societies Marx envisioned, where technology would benefit all and free each person to develop her or his maximum creative potential for the sake of all others. There remain dynamic Marxists who believe that Marx's method of historical analysis is relevant to the twentieth century, and who continue to be motivated by Marx's dynamics of historical hope. They have, however, achieved a new realism about the continuing alienation of persons in developed industrial societies, even those in socialist industrialized societies, after six centuries of trying to actualize his vision.

It is not our function as Christians to wish them ill in their struggle toward a genuinely human society, or to find joy in any frustration of their hopes up to now. It may be our function as historians to dispute at points their reading of history, or as economists to argue with their interpretation of data. As politicians or political scientists it may be incumbent upon us to contend with them for the merits of alternative political structures and processes, and as theologians to affirm and interpret alternative understandings of God, Christ and Churchh. It is never, however, our mission as Christians to do anything other than pray and work for the human fulfillment God in Christ intends for them. There simply can be no "dividing wall of hostility." When we discern a genuine commitment to justice and fulfillment for the poor, we should be grateful for possible allies in the work the Spirit of Christ gives to us.

To the degree that we as Christians cannot wholeheartedly love, pray and work for those we properly discern to be separated from us, we are the victims of ideology grounded in the national, racial and/or economic class anxieties and insecurities of our neighbors on this side of the wall. It is not surprising that we should in some ways share their ideology. We certainly share in their insecurities. What is surprising is that we do not pray, study, teach and learn more in order to transcend these ideological barriers to love and reason. No one can expect that a social wall will be easily breached when its historical foundations are so deep that Charlemagne put them in place and sections were built from the schism of 1054 between Eastern Orthodox and Roman Catholic Churches. Cemented by a millenia long struggle between Slavic and Germanic peoples for control of central Europe, it was capped by a struggle between capitalists with fascist tendencies and communists with totalitarian leanings. Though such a wall cannot be easily overcome in the social psyches of any of us, it has been overcome in the spiritual reality of Jesus Christ. We are called to participate in his victory.

49

It is remarkable that in the social history of the latter half of the twentieth century, the ideological fixations of North America, especially in the USA, have been symbolized by persons named "McCarthy." Senator Joseph McCarthy personified the virulent anti-communism of the 1950s, which lacked all appreciation of the Marxist commitment to justice for the poor. Senator Eugene McCarthy, despite the richer nuances of his perspective, symbolized for many Americans in the 1960s an ideological critique of North American society that did not properly assess the totalitarian dangers of communist power. Given the power of the mass media in the 1970s, North Americans were in danger of having the ventriloquist dummy, Charlie McCarthy, represent the passive, even apathetic, character of American social opinion, saying what it was manipulated to say by the opinion makers.

Let us pray that in the 1980s the churches of North America may ecumenically join the churches around the world as they enliven and inform their members about the realities of our global mission. The only proper symbol of our commitment is Jesus Christ, who overcomes every dividing wall of hostility.

Discussion Questions for Chapter 2

1. *What is and should be the Christian perspective on the political and economic "walls" that separate people by nation and ideology?*

2. *Is the way ecumenical organizations are seeking to make the unity of Christ's church visible crucial to mission? Can the Church be the Church anywhere without such ecumenical community?*

3. *Do North American Christians get enough information from the public media to make valid comparisons and judgments about eastern and western "blocs" in Europe? What is the responsibility of the churches to help bring more objective data to this dangerous ideological conflict that fuels the cold war and arms race?*

4. *Could Christian-Marxist dialogue have as useful an impact on North American churches in the 1980s as it did on European churches in the 1960s and Latin American churches in the 1970s? How can North American Christians overcome their stereotypes about Marxists and Communists?*

3. The Mission and Message of European Churches

In this chapter European Christians write directly about the situations in which they live and witness. What we have learned about the complexity of European church life indicates the importance of transcending North American perspectives by paying attention to what European sisters and brothers have to share. The four brief essays that follow offer accurate analyses of their situations and an authentic witness to their faith.

With space putting limits on what could be included, the following principles were used to determine the selection: 1) all three of the major Christian traditions should be represented: Orthodox, Protestant and Roman Catholic; 2) the nature and scope of their witness as revealed in a society where they constitute the majority church: Romania for the Orthodox, the German Democratic Republic for the Protestant, and Poland for the Roman Catholic; 3) the countries chosen to do this should be East European to continue the focus on this part of Europe, and thus expand the limited knowledge most North Americans have of that area; 4) the mission of West European churches should be expressed by authors who know both North America and Europe well, so that the vast possibilities in Western Europe are specifically addressed to a North American audience.

We are fortunate in the authors who agreed to write for us. Drs. Helga and Thomas Day have co-authored the rich essay on "Witness in Western Europe." Both have their Ph.D.s from Union Theological

51

Seminary in New York. Helga was born in the Federal Republic of Germany (West Germany) and now coordinates the Fraternal Worker Program for the Ecumenical Council in West Berlin. Thomas Day was born in Canada, taught ethics at Princeton Theological Seminary, and is now pastor to students at the Pädagogische Hochschule (College of Education) in West Berlin.

Dr. Albrecht Schönherr, author of "The Evangelical Churches in the German Democratic Republic" (translated by James Will), studied theology with Dietrich Bonhoeffer in the University of Berlin and the seminary of the Confessing Church in Finkenwalde. After founding and directing the seminary in Brandenburg from 1951-62, he became general superintendent in 1961 and bishop of the Church of Berlin-Brandenburg in 1972. He has served as chairperson of the Federation of Evangelical Churches in the German Democratic Republic since 1969.

The essay on the "Roman Catholic Church in Poland" was written by two professors from the University of Lublin, the only university under church auspices in Eastern Europe. Prof. Joachim Kondziela spent one year in the USA as a fellow of the East European Institute of Columbia University, New York. He now directs a Peace Research Center and teaches in the University of Lublin. His colleague, Prof. Wladyslaw Piwowarski, is one of the great authorities on the character of Polish religious life and the trends within it.

Bishop Vasile Tirgovisteanul, Assistant to the Patriarch and Director of the Department of External Church Relations, wrote the essay on "The Romanian Orthodox Church Today." Bishop Vasile directed the Romanian Orthodox mission in Jerusalem before assuming his present responsibilities.

Witness in Western Europe
Dr. Helga Day, Dr. Thomas Day

Americans struck with awe at the cathedrals of Europe may be struck with indignation when confronted with the bulky superstructures of our tax-fed churches. They seem so fat and fixed on self-preservation, so unresponsive to the needs of people, that is, the demands of the Gospel, in our upset age. A longer look, however, will show that behind the dark realities of our world a light burns, and the darkness has not overcome it. We intend to point to some of those places where the light shows through.

Toward the Priesthood of All Believers

One good result of the 1936 Olympics in Berlin was Black Jesse Owen's triumph in the arena of Aryan racism. Another was the first "Protestant Week" by means of which the Confessing Church was able to rally support. It was only possible because of the Gestapo's reluctance to cause public turmoil while all eyes were on Berlin. The Kirchentag (Church Assembly) and the Evangelical Academies are two major institutions of German Protestantism developing from this root. Through them were expressed hopes for a new beginning following the total collapse of church and society at the end of World War II.

Leaders like Martin Niemöller and Gustav Heinemann (later President of the Federal Republic of Germany) sought a fundamental renewal of the church growing out of living Christian communities. They were responsible for the establishment in October, 1945, of the Council of the Protestant Church in Germany and the Stuttgart Confession of the church's shared guilt in the horrible crimes of the German people during the years of Nazi rule. Their hopes for church unity and a new beginning were not to be realized, however. By 1949 it was clear to disappointed Christians that nothing had really changed. The restoration of the old church bureaucracy supported by the need for "peace and quiet" was winning ground everywhere.

To counter this retrogressive tendency, Gustav Heinemann, then president of the German Protestant Week, announced the founding of an annual "Kirchentag." It was intended "to prepare protestant laypeople for service in their parishes and the world as well as to further an exchange with laypeople of the churches of the World Council of Churches." Lay church members wanted to assume their proper role as equals in the bearing of church responsibility, to help the church break out of the ghetto into which it had let itself be pushed. They saw themselves in a strong position to bring Christian influence to bear in the world.

The Kirchentag was to be a new platform for encounter between theologians and laypeople, between members of the "Landeskirchen" and the smaller "free churches," between working class and middle-class people. In brief, it could be a crucible of creative unrest to combat the churches' stagnation. After 30 years the question must be asked whether the Kirchentag did overcome the limitations of middle-class "churchiness" and realize the apostolate of the laity.

Particularly since the beginning of the 1960s, the laity's role has been taken over to a great extent by professionals. The focus of the

Kirchentag, no longer the experience of community in the one Protestant Church of Germany, has shifted to questions of the role of the church in a fast-changing, pluralistic and insecure world. The participation of people from different social strata and professions—government ministers, union members, scientists, generals, economists and theologians—makes the Kirchentag an invaluable forum for the exchange of information and spontaneous expression. Intended to help Christians live responsibly in the world, it has succeeded in bringing many issues into local congregations and public discussion at large.

One area in which the Kirchentag has broken ground is Jewish-Christian Dialogue, a working group at each Kirchentag since 1961. Others include the open discussion of sexuality and, since 1965, a dialogue between Protestants and Catholics. The Protestant Kirchentag is now held every other year, with the Catholic church hosting a "Katholikentag" in the intervening years. At both, the worldwide ecumenical movement is represented by members of churches from all continents. As a result English dioceses now hold "Kirchentags" of their own, using the German name as a sign of reconciliation after two wars. Huge church assemblies open to all, they have assumed both an integrating and a critical, reforming function for the church in Germany. Many Christians not active in their local parishes take part in the Kirchentag because they find there possibilities of communication and information lacking in their local churches. Alongside traditional worship services, for instance, are "political night prayer," jazz masses, liturgical nights that combine elements of dance, prayer, song and the sharing of food and silence.

The Kirchentag's function as a place for experiment is particularly evident since 1975 in the "Market of Possibilities." Here diverse groups (over 400 in 1979) present their special concerns in provocative, sometimes shocking, ways. The Market, called "A World's Fair in a Sick World," is seen by some as *l'enfant terrible*, by others as the only adequate form for a living church. Mostly young people and women, participants try to sensitize their fellow Christians to issues like torture in Latin America, hunger in the Two-Thirds World, problems of alcoholics, convicts, orphans and such sensitive questions as the statute of limitations on Nazi crimes. At Kirchentag the priesthood of all believers is taken more seriously than is usual even in the Protestant churches.

Groups participating in the Market of Possibilities tend to develop continuity in their preparatory and follow-up work, which can have a

St. Mary's Church, East Berlin. "Approximately ten million citizens of the G.D.R. today are members of Christian churches and other religious communities."

renewing effect in their local churches. This requires that the local congregations practice at home the tolerance and variety they experience for 5 days every two years at the Kirchentag. The vitality and enthusiasm of the crowds at the Kirchentag still seem a long way from the sleepy, subdued Sunday morning church services, however.

Like the Kirchentag, the Evangelical Academies developed out of the "Protestant Week" that began during the Church's struggle against Nazi domination. Though under very different circumstances, they fulfill a similar function today. There are now 13 academies in the Federal Republic of Germany and West Berlin, which hold public meetings, extended seminars, encounters and continuing education programs. Study directors from different fields of expertise collaborate in interdisciplinary conversations. The participants are mainly working people and professionals between 25 and 55, precisely the age groups so under-represented among the active members of local churches. They come as employees of a concern, members of a profession, experts in a particular area, representatives of different political or social groups. The shape the encounters take depends on the specific theme and the participants. The goal is social learning, and personal experience is combined with objective information so that problems can be dealt with by those affected by and responsible for them. Lay persons and experts, handicapped and healthy people, theologians and representatives of other disciplines and professions meet for ecumenical and interdisciplinary dialogue. They experience what church can be like when Christians concentrate on the experiences and life situations of real people. The academies try to sharpen a Christian's perception of the social and political responsibilities arising from faith and to establish contact with those alienated from the church.

Social changes in the 30 years since the founding of the Evangelical Academies have caused major shifts in focus and increased criticism of the traditional forms of church organization. The level of expectation put upon the Kirchentag and academies also has risen, as society became more differentiated, professions tended to greater specialization and population mobility increased sharply. Changes in social values and norms have given rise to a new search for ethical orientation. As the legitimacy of certain social institutions is challenged, the academies often serve as "neutral ground" where hitherto antagonistic groups can enter new dialogue. For this reason they deal with many non-theological and non-ecclesiastical issues that are especially urgent in the society: women's liberation, social integration of handicapped persons, equality of educational opportunity, relationships with Germany's neighbors to the east, responsibility toward the Third World, antifascist education and reactions to the television film "Holocaust."

The Church long functioned as a counterpart to the state and society at large, providing space and enabling dialogue among conflicting parties in search of new alternatives. While it continues to fill a role of social mediation, its declarations and position papers on social issues, still too often couched in a terminology that is unintelligible to the person in the street, receive less and less notice. The Church is seen less as a counterweight to the state than as one association among many within the state. The general population can no longer be considered to be "Christian" in the way it once was. Like other European countries, the Federal Republic has become a missionary country, in which the vast majority of the population no longer feel themselves addressed by the church's message because its traditional forms are unable to deal with concrete life situation. Some 85 percent of nominal church members remain outside the communications network of their local parishes.

In this context the academies have tried to build bridges by providing a framework in which all people, regardless of church affiliation, can take initiative in defining their problems and searching for solutions. Christians and non-Christians reflect on their lives and discover common experiences. Alongside the official program there is room for individual conversations and a chance for pastoral counseling. Often the meaning of the Gospel can be expressed more clearly by laypeople telling of their attempts to be Christian in their political, cultural, workaday lives, than by the treatises of professional theologians. Living together during a conference provides an atmosphere in which prayer and worship, biblical reflection and the Eucharist take on deep significance. Here people can experience community through common experiences and interests, with as many as possible participating.

The academies try to live up to the church's claim that faith and life, praise of God and responsibility for the world belong together. They analyze how particular problems develop and initiate conversations with scientists, planners and politicians involved in them so that Christians can assume their share of responsibility. Through their search for adequate Christian life styles and forms of community life, the academies also offer help in dealing with history and environment, other people and various traditions. They provide a learning community and space for thinking new thoughts, developing new options and finding the courage to risk new experiences. They are institutions of adult education through which the "semper reformanda" church equips its members to live as Christians in our modern world.

Toward a Witness of Solidarity with the Poor

As lay initiatives, both the Kirchentag and the Evangelical Academies have been sources of experimentation and disquiet in the organized church. As such, they have been attacked by conservative church groups, rewarded with budget cuts and personnel changes designed to silence the critique and squelch the new forms of gospel proclamation. Other professional "disturbers" of the church are the mission organizations that keep Christians from lapsing into self-satisfied particularism. Fortunately, many people in West European churches have gone beyond the concept of "one-way mission" to the realization that the different churches throughout the world are members of the one body of Christ. They can learn from each other and support each other, even as each pursues its specific mission in its part of the world.

This ecumenical commitment was evident in the January, 1980, Report of the Protestant Mission Institute to the National Synod of the Protestant Church in Germany. In recent years the Mission Institute has tried to comprehend the situation of Third World churches against the background of the social, economic and political structures imposed upon them by our western life style and economic system. It has listened to Third World theologians who see the unity of the Church being denied by the unjust distribution of goods in the world, particularly among Christians. Faced with the crisis of world famine, the scarcity of natural resources and the waste of the arms race, the Mission Institute confronted the whole German church with the disquieting question of their own "way of life." It wanted the whole church to realize two things: first, to be truly concerned for ecumenical community, Christians must hear what others are saying and learn from them; second, Christians must accept the political, economic and social challenge posed by their brothers' and sisters' questioning of their life style, and ask whether or not that life style is a prophetic sign of Christian community and human solidarity.

The role poor people are understood to play in the history of salvation was taken seriously by the Protestant Mission Institute. The poor in grass roots Christian communities in the Third World have rediscovered themselves as the primary addressees of the Gospel and the bearers of Christian Mission and ask Western Christians if we want to be freed by the Gospel from being demonically possessed by our possessions. The Protestant Mission Institute's report reflects an attempt at this point to engage in mission as an ecumenical learning process. It seeks to learn from Third World Christians a more holistic understanding of mission and Christian existence. It concludes that if church experiments with new life styles are to be prophetic signs, they must be coupled with commitment to a new world economic order that requires a reorganization of western structures of production and consumption. A truly missionary church must have solidarity with the poor of the world. Christian love for all the members of Christ's Body cannot stop before existing political and economic structures. It must have the courage to identify the causes of poverty, hunger and injustice and go as far as it can to remove them.

As one might expect, this report was the object of vehement debate. Its authors were charged with being one-sided, exaggerating the social and political consequences of the Gospel and proposing justification by works instead of by faith. Though by a slim majority, the Synod rejected the report, giving the impression that they were more interested in supporting the status quo than in helping the materially poor and hungry. It appears that the leading bodies of the Protestant Church in Germany are not ready to let the church become the "instrument of re-thinking" that our society needs. Instead of taking sides biblically and heeding their own biblical motto for 1980, "God wants *all people* to be saved," they withdrew to a position of political neutrality.

Fortunately, such withdrawal is not true for the whole church in West Germany. In parishes throughout the land, and sometimes even at synods, there are groups of Christians who do not simply call "Lord, Lord ..." but take seriously Jesus' message of love for the impoverished and oppressed.

One example is the national "Protestant Women's Work," an organization made up of 43 Protestant women's groups, which in 1977 organized the boycott of South African fruit and produce. The boycott began as an act of solidarity with sisters in the "Black Women's Federation" in South Africa, one of 18 organizations banned by the Apartheid government for having tried to raise and change by peaceful means the consciousness of the Black population concerning their inhuman situation. The Protestant women in Germany hoped to awaken understanding for the situation of the Black people of South Africa and to support their struggle for justice and human dignity. Struck by the suffering of their Black sisters, they were not satisfied with only another declaration of solidarity. Convinced that prayer and practice, thought and action belong together, they began where they could, in their daily lives as shoppers, thereby signaling the total economic boycott of South Africa long since called for by the United Nations General Assembly. Without such measures the Apartheid regime will not give up the racist policies that blatantly contradict the justice of the God they confess.

Recognizing that the government of the Federal Republic of Germany, while doing lip service against racism, continues its economic and military support of the Apartheid system, the Protestant Women through their boycott take sides with the oppressed Black population to influence the situation in a nonviolent way. They also hope to inform the German public about the situation in South Africa and protest against the close economic, business and cultural cooperation between the Republic of South Africa and the Federal Republic of Germany.

The women have received support from groups concerned with the Third World, women's and youth groups and the Student Christian Movement. Only two official church bodies—the West Berlin Synod and the leadership of the North Elbian Church—have supported the call to boycott. The Rheinische Synode has also made a statement in support of the campaign. The National Council of the Protestant Church in Germany criticized the action and refused it any financial support!

Other churches in Europe have been more responsive to the call of the Nairobi meeting of the World Council of Churches to learn to see through the eyes of others. Those in Holland and Sweden, as well as the British Council of Churches, supported the boycott appeal and other economic sanctions against South Africa. They see such measures as among the last peaceful means of bringing about change there.

The Protestant women have also distributed widely informative materials, posters and slide shows. They have set up information stands in market places and supermarkets, held worship services and discussions in parishes, and staged theater presentations in the streets. Three nationwide boycott weeks were carried out in more than 50 cities. The boycott goes on, as Christian women try to act credibly. Knowing themselves to be members of one body with their sisters and brothers in South Africa, they are attempting to respond to their problems and suffering. While this brings them into conflict with some in their own church and society, they know that their Lord did not avoid conflict in questions of truth and justice.

Toward Grass Roots Community

A harsh experience for Christians during the Third Reich was that the Confessing Church stood firm only when the parish community remained resolute. Whenever clergy stood alone, they were powerless or soon removed. The church bureaucracy and synodal structures, controlled almost immediately by the pro-fascist "German Christians" and the "Neutrals" attempting to continue church business as usual without taking sides, were of little help. Effective resistance developed only at the parish level, where resolute congregations carried on, even after their pastors were arrested. This explains the new forms rising out of the "Church Struggle" from 1933-45, which focused on lay initiative in building responsible Christian communities. Impetus in the same direction is now coming like a boomerang from Christians in the Third World. In times past, European churches sent out missionaries to preach the Gospel of Jesus to the world's poor. Now poor Christians who heard that good news are preaching the Gospel's demands to overfed Europeans and calling for their conversion to the Gospel of the poor.

More responsive to this call than the national church structures are an increasing number of Christian groups in and around the churches. Some have long since left the pew. Others still sit in a far corner of the church. All are convinced that the church should be for people, not vice versa, that the Good News is about God's bringing justice to all, a task in which God requires our help. Most are trying to break out of a long tradition of other-worldly piety and clerical tutelage to a biblical solidarity. If they can do this within the institutional church, they do. But they leave it, if the church denies them the necessary space. They try to face up to the reality of their world in the light of Jesus' message by recognizing that to retreat into the Bible or mere political action is to give up the Holy Ghost.

The size of these groups ranges from "two or three together" to several hundred. They are egalitarian and ecumenical, though most of their members come from the Catholic tradition. Clergy are on an equal footing with all others. Some groups are breaking the class captivity of the churches by bringing together middle-class persons and migrant workers, for instance. In Holland some 80 diverse groups are joined in a support network with national and regional meetings, newsletters and even a tiny staff. In 1980 they refused an invitation to join the Dutch Council of Churches, lest their witness be set apart from the major churches as a new sect, easier for the church hierarchies to isolate and manage. They prefer to remain as biblical thorns in the flesh of the major churches.

One of the better known groups (too large to be typical) is the Critical Community of Ijmond in northwest Holland. Founded in a Catholic parish in the late 1960s, it gathers 600-700 persons every fortnight to celebrate the Eucharist in a rented Protestant church. The liturgical services reflect the concerns of the community's two dozen working groups: Peace Week, feminism, integration of the handicapped, refugees, the dumping of radioactive wastes in the North Sea, etc. The distribution of the 300-400 active volunteers in the different working groups contrasts greatly to the distribution found in the usual church:

Care Sector (Welfare Assistance, etc.)	*4 groups,*	*75 people*	
Social Action/Political Structures	*7 "*	*85*	*"*
Reflection/Discussion Groups	*6 "*	*100*	*"*
Liturgy Group/Choir	*5 "*	*130*	*"*
(includes many also in caring and			
social action groups)			
Internal Organization	*2 "*	*15*	*"*

Typically the larger grass roots communities function as coalitions of small groups with a minimum of superstructure.

In the small Calabrian town of Gioiosa Jonica in impoverished southern Italy a Christian community has occupied the parish church of St. Rocco since 1975 as part of their struggle against the domination of the Mafia and, unfortunately, the clergy. Traditional statues and paintings decorate the church along with fresh banners: "True Worship is a Life Engaged in Justice," "The Church Belongs to the People," and "To be a Christian Doesn't Mean Just to put Money on the Collection Plate!"

In a part of Brussels having a 70-80 percent immigrant population, a community of some 50 people work in small groups of three or four against the blatant racism they encounter. Their focus is on issues of housing, health, neglected old people and hapless new immigrants. Not all members are Christians. Some are Marxists or politically conservative, but they gather fortnightly to read the Bible with the help of Marxist social analysis and to celebrate the Eucharist.

As compared to the machinery and economic power of the major churches (the Protestant Church in West Germany is the biggest employer besides the federal government), these groups and hundreds like them seem insignificant. They are, however, cells of community in a society of isolated individuals and mass organizations. Their potential significance can be seen in the campaign of the Dutch Interchurch Peace Council, "Ban Nuclear Weapons from the World, Starting with Holland," in which grass roots communities are among 350 groups pledged to work for the next five to ten years to rid the world of nuclear weapons. In March 1978, 50,000 people took to the streets in Amsterdam. Within a few months, one-tenth of the entire population signed the petition against the neutron bomb. Polls show two-thirds of the Dutch against having nuclear weapons based in Holland, the broad basis helping explain why the Dutch government put up the toughest stand against the neutron bomb and Cruise and Pershing missiles being deployed in Europe. The churches' Peace Week every September focuses the issues and kicks off the effort of another season.

The Swedish churches also sponsor an annual "U-Week" (the Swedish words for "development" and "underdevelopment" both begin with the letter "u") on international justice and peace. Local church, union, youth, women's and other groups joined the first nationwide peace week initiated in West Germany by Action Reconciliation, a Christian organization of volunteer youth exchange with countries for whom Germany has been the aggressor.

In Europe, where wars have raged like prairie fires and an atomic thundercloud would mean "instant Auschwitz," small Christian communities are growing and spreading like new grass. Indeed, a light does burn, and the darkness has not overcome it.

The Evangelical Churches in the German Democratic Republic
Albrecht Schönherr

Preface (by Lutz Borgmann)

There are eight regional churches in the German Democratic Republic. Like those in the Federal Republic of Germany, they find their origin in the reformation of Martin Luther, and still take from the former small states of Germany the boundaries set by the Congress of Vienna in 1815.

It was in June 1969[1] that they formed the Federation of Evangelical Churches in order to create a "community of witness and service." Though a union of confessionally different and legally independent churches, the ministry and sacraments of all are recognized within the federation.

The organs of the Church Federation are the Synod, with 60 representatives from the regional churches, and the Conference of Evangelical Church Leaders. To accomplish the work common to all, a Secretariat with ten specialized commissions and committees has been created.

Approximately ten million citizens of the GDR today are members of Christian churches and other religious communities. About eight million of these are members of the Evangelical Regional Churches; 1.2 million belong to the Roman Catholic Church; the rest are members of Free Churches and other religious communities.

The population of the GDR in 1978 was 17.5 million, guaranteed by the constitution the right "to religious belief and action." Church and state are separated, and the churches administer their affairs independently within the laws of the GDR.

In April, 1979, Bishop Dr. Albrecht Schönherr, of the Evangelical Church of Berlin-Brandenburg, spoke to the synod of this body on the theme "The Mandate and Way of the Church of Jesus Christ in the Socialist Society of the GDR." The following is based on this lecture of Bishop Schönherr who has been chairperson of the Conference of Evangelical Church Leaders of the Federation of Evangelical Churches since 1969.

In the School of God

The path of the churches since the founding of the German Democratic Republic in 1949 has led through unexplored territory: for the first time a majority Protestant church has confronted Marxism-Leninism. Because socialism grounded on this world view is not limited to one particular party, but determines the entire state in which we live, the encounter is inescapable. With neither tradition nor model to follow on this path, it is no accident that we are asked again and again: Can one live as a Christian in a socialist society, as long as atheism is fundamental to Marxism-Leninism?

The answer may be derived only from the commission of the Church that bids us to declare to all: "I am the Lord, your God," and to invite all people to do what follows from this truth: "fear, love and trust God above all things." God cares for every single person and struggles in his world that this be recognized and accepted. Jesus has come just for this reason.

Our reflection about the way of the Church may not be divorced from this commission. That the Church is the fruit of this commission and lives to fulfill it is emphasized in the motto the Federation of Evangelical Churches chose for itself: "Community of Witness and Service." Because it has its commission from God, the freedom of proclamation is essential for the way the church must go in the world. For this reason it rejoices when it responsibly administers its own affairs and when Christians may freely live out what they believe. This also is why the Church is concerned for the entire world as God's creation, both as a whole and for every individual. It supports everything that promotes life and opposes what endangers it. The world that belongs to the Lord God must not be ruined by suffering, bloody conflict and pollution.

The church of Jesus Christ lives. We Christians live in the socialist society of the GDR. We thereby have new experiences and discover new possibilities. Our readiness to think, act and learn responsibly is demanded of us frequently. In the confidence that God faithfully supports those who place themselves in his service, we can understand this period as a school. The school of God.

The Possibilities of Smaller Congregations

The number of citizens in our land who call themselves Christian has become considerably smaller. In 1946 we could still count more than 16 million. Today, though we have no exact statistics, there are no more than 8 million in our Evangelical churches. (A similar numerical decline is found in most of the industrialized states of the northern hemisphere.) The national churches, which had created a unity of church and society, are involved in far-reaching change. At one time persons accepted their membership in the church and the church's place in the society and participated in the official activities of the church such as baptism, confirmation, weddings and funerals as a matter of course. Now, with smaller numbers, the need for these so-called official ministrations and the participation in churchly events, from worship services to religious education, is smaller.

The reasons for this decline range from the decline of village population (with the attendant uprooting from peasant tradition and customs) to the conviction that each is the maker of his or her own good fortune. Undoubtedly, the reasons do not lie primarily in atheist propaganda, as is clear when one compares similar phenomena in other states still having a Christian basis. What does that mean for the church? That as a minority, our faith is no longer a norm accepted as a matter of course, but one religious possibility among others. We are asked: "Why do you Christians persist? What do you really want?" The church, after all, can no longer expect the privileges accorded an uncontested majority. The pastors, no longer able to claim absolute authority as the guardians of generally recognized basic values, have lost a great deal of status in the social scale. Compare the per-month gross income of a pastor that presently falls between 600-800 marks with the 900 marks per month the average factory worker earns.

But is this really so bad? Isn't it even good that we Christians now must think seriously about our faith, must give a "reason for the hope that is in us" (1 Peter 3:15)? Have we not often suffered in the past from the disinterest and indifference of many? Surely, it is a good sign that questions about baptism, confirmation, communion and marriage are vigorously discussed, and a great opportunity that the preacher of the gospel may no longer be content to make the generally recognized facts of faith palatable, but must show quite concretely the importance of the gospel in life. It is a good thing when pastors and all other church workers enjoy a deeply rooted trust. There is the possibility that the small minority congregation can give a clearer witness to its faith than a church concerned with keeping the support of a majority.

These new possibilities are recognized only with pain. The small numbers with the related decrease in financial power means, for example, that we must reconsider how to fill all the pastoral offices. Should we concentrate on the work of the pastor, who still is understood to be the most important ecclesiastical officer? Or shall we struggle to maintain a variety of church professions? As far as our church is concerned we believe that we dare not wait only for the growth in pastoral vocations, but must develop new possibilities: the use of qualified lay volunteers, readers, graduates of church correspondence courses. For example, the Evangelical Churches in the GDR prepare the laity for the ministry of preaching through seminars or correspondence courses which when successfully completed qualify one to preach the Word freely in the churches. Alternate simple and festive worship services are planned in order to gather the small community around one table and into larger church celebrations.

The small congregation, if it escapes a ghetto mentality, has the choice of becoming a support community of fellowship and pastoral care that shares security, comfort and advice with persons who try to live their faith in their daily lives, and who must answer when they are asked about it.

Political Responsibility

Faith engages the whole life of each person. Therefore, Christians are motivated to practice political responsibility, also. This contradicts the long-held belief that it was inappropriate, even impious, for Christians to concern themselves with political questions. Politics, it was believed, not only spoiled one's character, but destroyed the peace of the congregation. But what kind of peace is it that excludes large and essential areas of life? The experience of our older generations has taught us that Hitler was successful not least because Protestants were too credulous, too dependent on authority and too politically inexperienced. This example alone shows the danger of retreating to an unpolitical "pure" piety. By assuming a passive political position, we help those who know all too well how to use it for their purposes.

To think in terms of an "unpolitical Christian" is therefore a dangerous illusion. How can people have faith without counting on God's working in the world? How can people love without helping those who suffer under political injustice and oppression? How is it possible to hope without working toward a politically healthier world? We Christians must proclaim the peace of God—the peace expressed as "shalom" in the Old Testament that is not only peace in our hearts but one that comprehends the whole of life. It means not only a healed relationship between God and persons, but between person and person, and between persons and the creation. It is hypocrisy to view the lack of peace in our world as the "regrettable" norm to justify leaving the making of peace entirely to God. In the same way, it is hypocrisy to "regretfully" ignore sickness and hunger in the world, claiming that only the future Kingdom of God will bring conclusive help.

Precisely because we know what God wills in his Reign of Peace, we have the opportunity and the duty here and now to "make peace" (Mt. 5:9). This means taking small steps toward earthly peace, knowing full well they will be limited and incomplete.

We are glad to be able to study world peace in the context of the ecumenical movement and, upon occasion, to contribute to peaceful developments. Though not a government with the kind of power only governments possess, we nevertheless can make an immediate contribution to peace as we work for "inner disarmament." We must make clear to ourselves and others that no state or group of states may automatically and for all time be seen as the enemy; people dare not expect that solutions to political questions will inevitably come from military action rather than peaceful negotiations. In an effort that we call "peace education" in our churches, we must learn how to resolve conflicts peacefully in our neighborhoods, families, jobs and congregations. It must be repeatedly emphasized that education for peace remains an unconditional priority for us, even though military instruction has been introduced in our schools despite our objections.[2]

Responsibility for peace is closely related to responsibility for justice. No peace effort that ignores justice can succeed. Therefore, it was necessary that our churches affirm the World Council of Churches' Program to Combat Racism, a program that is a special case for the application of human rights. The correlation between peace and human rights can no longer be ignored since the Helsinki Final Act.[3] While human rights formulae are not directly derived from the Bible, we Christians affirm them as the appropriate expression of the dignity of human persons in our historical epoch. It is our conviction that this dignity is not grounded in the person as such, but in God's having created humanity "in his image" to be his partner. It is a permanent task to assess carefully the balance between the rights of the general public, in which the well-being of the individual is protected, and the rights of the individual, which affirm his or her uniqueness in relation to the group. We Christians should follow our Lord in thinking and working for the rights of others before our own.

To Live Responsibly in a Socialist Society

If God's free grace is the ultimate reality in this world, nothing can separate us from the love of God. Thus we need not react anxiously or maliciously to any people in our society, even if they are not Christian. Rather, we can live responsibly, circumspectly, and helpfully even in a socialist society. Dietrich Bonhoeffer helped us learn this when he wrote from prison in 1944:

> It will not be difficult for us to renounce our privileges, recognizing the justice of history. We may have to face events and charges that take no account of our wishes and our rights. But if so, we shall not give way to embittered and barren pride, but consciously submit to divine judgment, and so prove ourselves worthy to survive by identifying ourselves generously and unselfishly with the life of the community and the sufferings of our fellow persons.[4]

To be sure, the difficulty remains that Christians cannot agree with all the perceptions and ideas of Marxism-Leninism. Responsible representatives of the Evangelical Church as early as 1958 declared that they respected the development toward socialism in the GDR, and wanted to contribute to the peaceful construction of the life of their people. Ten years later, the Evangelical bishops stated in relation to the draft of a new constitution: "As citizens of a socialist state we understand ourselves to have the task of actualizing socialism as a more just form of living together. We are reminded as Christians that we have neglected to a great extent in Christendom the concerns of the poor and the disenfranchised, ignoring the implications of the gospel of God's coming reign." In the meetings of the Synod of the Church Federation during the first year after its founding in 1969 the question of its place in and perspective on society was often the center of discussion. The following formulation comes from the second meeting of the Synod in 1970:

> We shall experience the entire fullness of the freedom to which God called us in Jesus Christ only when we place our whole lives in his service. God thereby turns us toward other people, not only in the private sphere, but also in society and politics. Christ makes us responsible for all— for the city and for the state in which we live. We shall mutually have to help each other to fulfill the tasks which this responsibility brings us. What we do and how we do it

should point to Christ who has taken us into his service. Above all, we shall have to help each other transmit the gospel to the people of our time as a joyful, liberating message and not as burden and law.

At the next Synod meeting in 1971, the following formula was devised: "We want to be a church not along side of, and not against, but we want to be a church *in* socialism." This statement rejects a ghetto existence for the church, or its existence as an opposition party or a counter-society. To be a church *in* socialism means, first, the presence of the church where its members live and work; second, participation in the problems and achievements of the society, and responsibly contributing to its development. But it also means preservation of the independence that derives from the church's mission. The Church of Jesus Christ can never become a church *of* socialism. "A church in socialism" is a formula which should help us avoid: first, the danger of complete accommodation by a church that has become powerless and therefore is tempted to sacrifice the freedom and fullness of its proclamation for the "pottage" of a greater chance of survival; second, the danger of total rejection, resting on the false conviction that a regime that is basically atheistic and totalitarian can only bring forth evil, always and everywhere.

The formula "a church in socialism" has also been accepted by our state. The necessary precondition was the development of a state policy toward the church, which, after phases of uncertainty (because they too had no precedents) and a rigid ideological attitude, made a new beginning with the remarkable statement that Christianity and the humanistic goals of socialism are not in opposition to each other.[5] Paul Verner, a member of the Central Committee of the Socialist Unity Party (Communist), gave a speech in 1971 elaborating the practical consequences of this position. He recognized the independence of the church and its autonomy in issues of organization and personnel. He also acknowledged religion as such as a motivation for positive social developments. In the subsequent discussions between representatives of the churches and the state we have again and again emphasized the meaning of the Christian faith for the whole of society. From among many possible examples where our claim apparently has been accepted I mention only: our diaconic work as an especially valuable contribution of the church to society; efforts for peace in connection with the work of the World Council of Churches;

the work following the Helsinki Conference on Security and Cooperation in Europe; our efforts for environmental protection and disarmament; our contributions toward the construction of the Polish Pediatric Center in Warsaw, as a memorial for the Polish children who died in World War II.[6]

The pledge given in 1976 to allow new church buildings to be built in new housing districts was important not only as church policy but at an ideological level. It implied the conviction that there will be people for a long time to come who will confess and practice their Christian faith.

All these developments contributed to the meeting between the chairman of the Council of State of the GDR, Erich Honecker, and the executive committee of the Conference of Evangelical Church Leaders on March 6, 1978. At this time the social significance and the right to full social participation of the churches was recognized, without any effort to make them into "socialist mass organizations." The independence of the churches was expounded. Christian citizens were guaranteed equal opportunity and equal respect as "an obligatory norm." The churches proposed that the experiences of individual Christians in their various localities should be the measure for the relationships between church and state.

This official discussion sought to create the basis for the cooperation of Christians and non-Christians in shaping the future. The churches in the GDR desire that this cooperation be more than a cool proximity or a laboriously maintained tolerance, that it go beyond the traditional standpoints on both sides by an increased effort to understand and respect each other out of their own histories and convictions.

The history of the relations between Christianity and socialism is burdened with painful experiences on both sides. It would be good if after a generation of being together in one state, our historical memory would be enriched with new and good experiences. This is important not only for the relation of church and state, and between Christians and non-Christians, but for the future and survival of the world.

Section Notes

1. The eight regional churches are: the Evangelical Church of Anhalt, the Evangelical Church in Berlin-Brandenburg, the Evangelical Church in the Görlitz Church Region, the Evangelical Church of Greifswald, the

Evangelical-Lutheran Church of Mecklenburg, the Evangelical Church of the Church Province of Saxony, and the Evangelical-Lutheran Church in Thüringen. The Unity of Brothers (Moravian) District of Herrnhut is also a member of the Federation.

2. Compulsory military instruction was introduced into the curriculum for the 9th and 10th classes of the general education Upper Schools in the GDR in 1978. The churches expressed their opposition a number of times, arguing that the previous peace policy of the GDR could thereby become discredited in the world. As a positive answer to this military instruction, the churches developed a program of "Education for Peace."

3. The responsibility of the churches for peace has recently become clear in the discussions with the National Council of Churches of Christ in the USA on the issues of disarmament (1978 and 1979), through the participation of church representatives in the special session of the World Peace Council, February, 1979, in Berlin; in the publication of "Word for Peace" together with the Evangelical Churches in the Federal Republic of Germany on the occasion of the 40th anniversary of the beginning of the Second World War; and the "Declaration of the Evangelical Churches in the GDR concerning the Present World Political Situation" of January, 1980.

4. Dietrich Bonhoeffer (1906-1945), evangelical theologian and resistance fighter, who was executed in a concentration camp. The quotation is from his *Letters and Papers from Prison (Widerstand und Ergebung)*.

5. Walter Ulbricht, chairman of the Council of State, April 10, 1960.

6. Christians in the Evangelical and Free Churches in the GDR gave more than 1.5 million marks for the furnishing of the "Health Center for Children" in Warsaw. In addition, youth groups helped with the construction of the hospital.

Roman Catholic Church in Poland
Joachim J. Kondziela,
Wladyslaw F. Piwowarski

The Roman Catholic Church in Poland is worthy of interest not only because a Pole has been elected Pope for the first time in history. The primary reason is that for over 35 years it has functioned within a socialist Marxist-Leninist system while maintaining its vitality in the life of individuals and the nation, as well as preserving its influential social position. This leads us to reflect on its present character, the contemporary and historical factors conditioning its mission in its society, and recent church-oriented changes in Polish religious life.

General Information About the Church in Poland

Poland's present boundaries comprise 312,677 square kilometers, inhabited by over 35 million people of Polish nationality. There are no detailed religious statistics in contemporary Poland but, on the basis of various sources, we may assume that the religious-denominational structure is as follows: over 90 percent are Catholic, including about 1 percent who are Greek Catholics; 2-3 percent are Orthodox or Protestant (with the Orthodox having many more members than the Protestant churches); the much smaller membership of other sects and religions. The rest of the population consists of non-religious people, although most of these have been baptized.

The Roman Catholic Church is divided administratively into 27 dioceses with 77 bishops (both ordinaries and subsidiaries), 706 decantes (each consisting of some dozen or so parishes), 7,556 parishes (of which 72.9 percent are rural, 17.7 percent rural-urban and 9.4 percent urban parishes). The present ministry of the Roman-Catholic Church in Poland has 10,531 parish and auxiliary church buildings and 1,682 chapels. Since World War II, 538 new churches have been built, 871 churches destroyed during the war were rebuilt, and 101 new chapels erected. Of 20,298 Roman Catholic priests in Poland, 15,305 are diocesan and 4,893 monastic. This means one priest for every 1,500 Catholics.

The Roman Catholic Church in Poland is known for its high level of vocations for the ministry. At the present time, there are 4,179 candidates in 25 diocesan seminaries and 1,666 in 25 monastic seminaries. It is notable that in Poland the number of vocations for the ministry continues to increase: in 1971 there were 3,097 candidates for priests in diocesan seminaries, and 991 candidates in monastic seminaries; in 1979 the number has increased by 1,082 and 675 respectively. A similar growth can be seen in the number of ordinations: 480 priests (356 diocesan and 124 monastic) ordained in 1971; an increase in 1970 to 589 newly ordained priests (407 diocesan, and 182 monastic). There are 42 convents for men and 102 convents for women, distributed across Poland in 2,588 establishments. Besides the monastic priests noted above, monastic congregations include 1,501 friars. There are 25,712 nuns in the women's convents. Engaged in missionary work in Africa, Latin America, Asia and Oceania are 731 priests, 280 nuns, 45 friars and eight lay Catholics.

Due to a state ban there are no religious organizations or schools in

Poland. Children from elementary and secondary schools are taught religion in 11,596 catechetical stations organized by the church. Of these, 2,316 are located in churches, 1,212 in chapels, 4,597 in buildings adjacent to churches and 3,471 in private houses. Religion lessons are attended by over 90 percent of all the children who have not yet received there first Holy Communion. In the higher elementary grades the percentage drops to 50 percent, and in secondary schools, to 30 percent.

There no longer are theological faculties in the state universities in Poland, but about 2,500 students, both clerical and lay, attend the Catholic University of Lublin, a private school with university rights accepted by the state. Another graduate religious school is the Academy of Catholic Theology, where about 1,700 students, priests and laymen study. In addition there are four papal philosophical-theological faculties with a small number of students, most of whom are priests.

The Roman Catholic Church in Poland has its own press, though the circulation is too small to satisfy all its needs. A special lack is a Catholic newspaper. There are, however, three Catholic weeklies with a combined circulation of 192,200, as well as monthlies, bi-monthlies, quarterlies and annuals, all with relatively low circulation. There is also a press published by the Catholics who are grouped in PAX and the Christian Social Association. It is worth noting that PAX publishes the daily "Słowo Powszechne" with a circulation of 95,000 copies on week days and 200,000 on Sundays.

Historical and Contemporary Conditioning of the Activity of the Church

As this data makes clear, the Roman Catholic Church remains an important social force in Poland, although it does not have at its disposal entirely satisfactory institutional means for influencing its society. There are nevertheless a number of factors favorable for its evangelical mission in the Polish nation. The following seem to be the most important.

a) *The identification of the Roman Catholic Church with the Nation*. The Church was actively present at the beginning of the Polish nation and has continued to be throughout its history, supplying and defending nation-creative values. Its creative and sustaining presence was especailly clear in the periods when Poland was divided into provinces (twelfth and thirteenth centuries) and partitioned between three bordering states (from the eighteenth to twentieth centuries). In those times the church played a broad, integrative function as a symbol of national identity and independence. The saying "to be a Pole means to be a Catholic" originated in those difficult times. In contrast to the situation in some other nations, the church in Poland did not identify itself with particular social classes, but with the whole nation.

Identification with the nation, however, did not mean identification with the state. There were periods in the history of the Polish nation, as during the German invasion of Poland, when there was no independent state but the nation existed with the church as a symbol of its unity. This role has given the church high prestige in the whole nation and the confidence of all the people, regardless of their degree of involvement in religious life. It has become an integral component of national culture and the basis of national identity.

b) *The Role of the Family in Transmitting and Supporting Religious Life.* Because there are no religious organizations or schools in Poland, the family plays a particularly important role in transmitting and supporting religious values and behavior. This is especially true in an extended family, composed of representatives of several generations. Despite housing hardships, this type of family is still relatively common in Poland, in both the country and the cities. Because of the extermination of the urban population during the German occupation, the cities after the war were populated with people of rural origin, and rural religiosity penetrated the whole of the Polish society. Within this type of religiosity is found the phenomenon of "inherited" religion, where religious values are transmitted from one generation to another along with the whole cultural heritage. The family appears to be the main factor contributing to the continuity of religious tradition in the Polish nation.

c) *The Specific Role of the Socialist System in Poland.* Paradoxically, the socialist system in Poland, despite its atheistic assumptions, is a factor favorable for the maintenance of traditional and church-oriented religiosity because it stresses satisfying the basic needs of the society and minimizes individual consumerism. (The practical materialism of the consumption-oriented way of life in the highly developed societies of Western Europe is apparently a most unfavorable factor for institutional and traditional religiosity.) To be sure, religion is constantly threatened by an officially preferred materialistic outlook on life, the propagation of which aims a blow at national values, especially religious values. This has led to a certain opposition against such socializing forces because of the common tendency to maintain the national culture intact and continuous.

d) *The Specific Role of the Church in the Polish Situation.* In Poland there is very little of the kind of pluralism found in western countries that is created by many autonomous groups and institutions preferring their own values and patterns of cultural behavior. In Poland there are only two ideological systems, the Roman Catholic Church and the state. All other existing social structures are subordinated. This situation creates favorable conditions for both ideologies to influence the society as a whole. In spite of limited resources, the church continues to play its integrative role for the nation, and resists the negative effects of imposed secularization. Consequently, a dominant activity of the church is mass ministry in the national tradition, which with considerable success keeps masses of believers within the church. The signs of such success are mass participation in religious practices, overcrowded churches on feasts, emotional bonds between Catholics and parishes and the church, and the confidence in the church hierarchy, among others.

As a result of the four factors mentioned above, Poland's particular type of religiosity has been maintained on a relatively high level.

Changes in Traditional and Church-Oriented Religiosity

Public opinion polls in Poland reveal that attitudes toward the faith have not changed on a large scale. In 1968, there were 86.6 percent deeply involved believers. Ten years later the situation was almost the same, with the polls showing 86.4 percent. The small remaining percentage consists of religiously indifferent persons and nonbelievers. The group of nonbelievers in this Marxist-Leninist state is particularly interesting because it comprises only 5-7 percent of the total population. This means that forces promoting atheism are not major factors creating change in Poland, that religious tradition does persist. However, there is some question about changes within religiosity itself.

Although the index of believers in Poland remains high, there are clear trends toward the abandonment of church and tradition-oriented religiosity. Research carried out during the last 20 years by various church and state centers shows that changes have occurred in two directions. The first is the tendency to deepen religious life within the model of traditional religiosity preserved by the church, which characterizes only about 10 percent of the Polish population. This consists in experiencing the sacred as a personal value, in conscious involvement in the life of the church and in binding religion with everyday life. Among the people moving in this direction are about 5,000 older people, who experience religion in communes of neocatechumenates, and some 50,000 young people in communes called "oases."

The more common tendency, which is toward selective religiosity, is represented by over 30 percent of the population, and characterized by only partial identification with the church. Though these persons declare themselves as believers and Catholics who practice more or less frequently, they neither adhere unconditionally to the doctrine of the church (the dogmas of the faith and moral principles), nor fully submit to its guidance. They tend to dismiss external participation in the life of the church, selectively forming their attitudes under the influence of a pluralistic culture in an industrial society rather than that of atheistic propaganda. This new social form of religiosity is still neither clear nor homogeneous. The rest of the population represents the traditional, church-oriented religiosity characterized by a deep emotional attachment to the "faith of the fathers," ritualism, and the church's hierarchy.

Tendencies toward change, particularly the one toward selective religiosity, are especially common among young people, men, persons performing highly specialized jobs and those with higher education.

These facts about the Roman Catholic Church in Poland show that even in a socialist state of the Marxist-Leninist type the church continues to have the possibility of influencing society. What is more, specific conditions in such a society enable it, despite limited means, to exert its influence on a wide scale because of its relation to the continuing national-religious tradition. The major achievements of the church thus far are particularly visible in the sphere of the institutional-church, such as fulfilling the integrative function for the whole society, opposing the influence of imposed secularism and fulfilling the socio-critical function. It does not seem, however, that the church in Poland influences the attitudes of Catholics or deepens religious consciousness to a satisfactory extent. This suggests a certain danger for the future of the church and religion in Poland, unless the forms of pastoral activity are improved.

(Top) Outside mass, Church at Nowa Huta, Poland. "The Roman Catholic Church in Poland continues to have the possibility of influencing society."
(Bottom) The COZIA Monastery, Olt Valley, Romania. "Many places of worship throughout Romania stand as signs of the century-old spirituality of the Romanian people.

The Romanian Orthodox Church Today
Bishop Vasile Tirgovisteanul

The Christian teaching among Romanians is of apostolic origin, in the preaching of St. Andrew the Apostle. A great many historical vestiges and archeological findings confirm the early penetration of Christianity into the territory of Romania. One can say beyond doubt that the Romanians were born a Christian nation. There have been preserved to this day names of bishops and archbishops who lived on the territory of our land as early as the fourth century.

In spite of the barbarian invasions that swept over their territory, the Romanian people have remained unshaken in their fatherland. This confirms an old Romanian saying: "Waters run by but stones stay."

The most important events in the building up of the Romanian Church organization are linked with the development of the state. The formation of the Romanian Principalities is related to the setting up of the respective metropolitan centers of the church in the fourteenth century. Modern Romania was formed in 1918, and the Romanian Church, proclaimed a self-governing (autocephalous) national Patriarchate in 1925.

The Romanian Orthodox Church is a national church. Through its presence in the life of the Romanian people it has contributed to the very preservation of the Romanian people, the defense of the Romanian land and the activation of the Romanians' aspirations for unity and national independence.

Religious Denominations in Romania and Their Relation to the State

In Romania there are 14 religious denominations, including the Romanian Orthodox Church. Although the membership of the Orthodox Church comprises 80 percent of all the faithful in the land, it has no special privileges. All denominations in Romania are equal before the law, with equal rights and obligations. Christian or non-Christian, each preserves its specific doctrine and organizational structures.

Article 17 of the Constitution of the Socialist Republic of Romania guarantees all Romanian citizens civil and religious rights. It does not discriminate on grounds of race, sex or religion. Citizens enjoy equal rights in all the fields of life: economics, politics, justice and culture. Article 30 guarantees liberty of conscience to all, with each citizen free to accept or not a religous faith. In addition, freedom of worship is guaranteed. Religious denominations in Romania are recognized by the law and can organize themselves and function freely. The rights and obligations of the faithful fall into the vast category of general rights of all citizens of the land.

The relationships between the state and the Romanian Orthodox Church are based upon the church's full autonomy to establish administrative and practical structures in accordance with its traditions. The faithful practice in accordance with their own doctrine and traditions.

The Organization of the Romanian Orthodox Church

The Romanian Orthodox Church is headed by a Patriarch, elected by the National Church Assembly, whose large membership includes a delegate of the government, a delegate of the parliament and one from the Department for Religious Affairs. On June 12, 1977, His Beatitude Dr. Iustin Moisescu was elected Patriarch.

The Romanian Patriarchate organizes and functions on the basis of the *Statutory Rules for Organization and Functioning*, adopted by the Holy Synod in 1948, and amended according to the development of the life of the church. The activity of all departments is regulated by 12 bodies of separate rules.

The Romanian Orthodox Church has about 8,100 parishes, each with one to three priests. The total number of priests is about 10,000. The parishes in each diocese are organized into deaneries *(protopopiates)*. Each deanery has about 80-120 parishes, and is headed by a *protopop* (dean) whose business it is to supervise the physical, administrative and pastoral work of the priests. The highest authority in spiritual, canonical and general church affairs is the Holy Synod. Its members are: the Patriarch as president, all the metropolitans, archbishops, bishops, bishop assistants to archbishops and assistant bishops.

The Bible and Missionary Institute

The Romanian Patriarchate, in order to develop a missionary work adequate to the religious needs of the faithful, set up a Bible and

Orthodox Missionary Institute. It synchronizes the editorial work and the central workshops of the Patriarchate. The Printing House of the Patriarchate in Bucharest prints the central church journals, books for the ritual, theological books, monographs of church art, albums, wall calendars, icons, and so forth. Under the direction of His Beatitude Patriarch Iustin, the publishing house prints studies that help priests in their missionary and pastoral duties, including works of the Holy Fathers in Romanian translation that are so necessary for both the clergy and the church in general.

For current missionary needs the Romanian Patriarchate has developed its own central workshops: the weaving mill of Ţigăneşti convent that, with a section for embroidery and carpets, produces materials for church vestments; four workshops in the convent of Pasărea for church tailoring and small metal work such as crosses and medallions in filigree and enamel. At the monastery of Plumbuita three workshops craft church bells, wood-carvings and other wood-work. Other Patriarchate workshops function elsewhere to assist the development of a normal religious life specific to the Orthodox Church. All dioceses have their own publishing houses and candle workshops.

Religious Assistance for Romanian Orthodox Abroad

Besides the missionary work developed for the benefit of the faithful within the national boundaries, the Romanian Patriarchate has initiated an Orthodox mission addressed to the spiritual requirements of the Romanian Orthodox who live outside of Romania. His Beatitude Patriarch Iustin, together with the members of the Holy Synod and central church bodies, see to it that all members of the Romanian Orthodox Church living abroad are assisted as they seek to keep alive the sacred flame of faith in their new surroundings. Thus, in order to strengthen their unity of faith with the mother-Church, priests are sent to them when they request it, as well as church chanters, vessels and vestments when needed, salaries for the clergy, funds to cover the expenses of parish houses and the maintenance of churches. The Romanian State also provides for the necessary exchange in currency to take care of the Romanian Orthodox communities abroad. In this way parishes, such as those in Australia and New Zealand that dedicated places of worship in 1980, are able to build new church buildings.

Churches and Monastic Settlements
of Historical Importance

Many places of worship throughout Romania stand as signs of the centuries-old spirituality of the Romanian people. The most precious jewels of the Romanian Orthodox Church, they witness to centuries of vital religious life.

Over the last 30 years such "historical monuments" used by the church for worship have been restored through the combined efforts of the diocesan centers and the faithful and, in many cases, massive financial support from the Romanian State.

Returned to their original beauty, many shelter collections of icons and other church objects of inestimable artistic and historical value. They are visited by great numbers of believers, who are inspired to greater religious strength and zeal for the preservation of the historic faith.

Theological Education

The theological education in the Romanian Orthodox Church takes place in special schools on the secondary and university level. No religious denomination, however, may open educational institutions except as schools for training their clergy.

Removed from the tutelage of the state in 1948, Romanian Orthodox theological schools are under the direction of the Holy Synod and the local bishops. In this way they have been greatly improved for the pastoral and missionary objectives of the clergy. Year by year the curriculum better corresponds to the needs of the church. The training of church chanters lasts two years. It is carried out alongside the training for the priesthood, by the same teaching staff of each theological seminary.

Theological seminaries offer the students five years of theological training as well as subjects of general education. Their graduates qualify for the priesthood. Usually the ordinands continue their higher theological education in the Theological Institutes, on a part-time basis if ordained and working in parishes. There are six theological seminaries in the Romanian Patriarchate. Each enrolls on the average of 250-300 students.

The Theological Institutes in Bucharest and Sibiu, each with four years of study, confer academic degrees on their graduates. They enroll approximately 1500 theological students annually. In general, the number of graduates corresponds to the annual needs for church personnel. Those with the best qualifications may specialize further in one or another theological discipline that aims toward a doctor's degree in theology.

Many Romanian theological students pursue their specialities in theological faculties abroad. In the last few years 94 theological students of the Romanian Orthodox Church were awarded ecumenical scholarships or were on exchange. Many theological students from abroad study in our Theological Institutes.

Formerly a professor of Biblical Theology, the present Patriarch of the Romanian Orthodox Church joins his rich teaching experience with a profound understanding of the religious realities gained as leader of our church. Due to His Beatitude's concern, theological education in the Romanian Orthodox Church has acquired professors with solid theological training received both in Romania and abroad. His Beatitude has adjusted the curriculum in order to secure for the future priests of the Romanian Orthodox Church a preparation that corresponds to the realities of the contemporary world in which they will function as pastors. The exchange of theological students not only broadens the horizons of knowledge but is a means for building closer relations with the various Christian Churches.

Refresher Missionary Courses and Deanery Conferences for the Clergy

The Romanian Orthodox Church has for a long time offered refresher missionary and pastoral courses for the clergy. These are intended to up-date the theological knowledge of the clergy and acquaint priests with new developments in the general Christian and international life, the evolution of the relationships between church and society, as well as with tasks lying ahead for the Romanian Orthodox clergy. Such courses generally are held each year and are attended by each clergyman every five years. During the month they last, attending priests share their own pastoral experiences.

The deanery conferences are twofold: doctrinal and practical, or *orientative* and *administrative*. The first type deals with themes of general church interest, especially the ecumenical life of Christendom, internationally or locally. They are held four times a year. The *administrative conferences* are held twice a year in each deanery and deal with financial aspects, relationships with church and lay authorities, parish councils and committees, and so forth. In all these conferences the Holy Synod introduces with each theme interesting new material that will be useful for the active engagement of the clergy in the service of the church and the world.

Theological Publications

The theological press in the Romanian Orthodox Church issues a number of journals, including three central journals published by the Patriarchate in Bucharest. The Department for Church Foreign Relations publishes a quarterly journal "Romanian Orthodox Church News" in English and French. Each of the five metropolies publishes its own journal and the Metropolia of Ardeal also brings out the church newspaper "Telegraful Român." A number of the 13 dioceses publish yearly an "Indrumător Pastoral" (Pastoral Almanac). All aspects of the church life, internal and external, are touched upon by these publications. Each month approximately 1,000 pages are published.

Many bulletins, journals and almanacs are produced by the Romanian Orthodox communities abroad. The Publishing House of the Bible Institute in Bucharest prints manuals for theological students or to meet any other requirements.

In this way, as well as through the church services, sermons and catecheses and direct relationship between the clergy and the faithful, the Romanian Orthodox Church successfully develops her missionary activity in the service of the faithful. A special commission for church painting and architecture attached to the Patriarchate supervises and guides approximately 400 church painters. The churches, whether with one or two priests, are always open for the faithful.

Ecumenism

The Romanian Orthodox Church seeks to develop the best relations with both the Christian Churches and non-Christians, such as Jews and Muslims, living in Romania. Every denomination makes its contribution to the welfare of the new society in Romania, and the building of a new world of justice, equality and freedom. In this area the churches and denominations develop friendly relationships among themselves.

Thus, every year two or three ecumenical theological conferences are held, in which Orthodox, Roman Catholics and Protestants take part. Such conferences are hosted in turn by the Theological Institutes of Bucharest, Sibiu and Cluj. Sometimes their themes focus on practical ecumenism—cooperation among the religious denominations in Romania and their relationships with the contemporary world. Or they may be purely theological, seeking theological consensus for Christian unity. The denominations may meet in consultations to express their common religious stand on contemporary internal and external problems. Delegates and representatives of the Romanian Orthodox Church are always present at festivities occasioned by events in the life of the other religious denominations in Romania, as non-Orthodox, and even non-Christian, delegates are present at Romanian Orthodox festivities. All these manifestations are proof of an understanding and collaboration that are pleasing to God.

In the field of external relationships, the Romanian Orthodox Church develops a wide ecumenical activity that helps build friendly relationships with the other Christian churches and inter-Christian or international organizations supporting the contemporary aspirations of the world toward rapprochement, collaboration and peace among humankind and nations.

An important step toward harmonious relations was taken by the Romanian Orthodox, together with the other Orthodox churches, through inauguration in 1980 of official Orthodox-Roman Catholic theological dialogue. The relationships of the Romanian Orthodox Church with other Christian denominations also are being continually deepened. In all these contacts, the ecumenical openness of the Romanian Orthodox Church, under the leadership of His Beatitude Patriarch Iustin with the members of the Holy Synod, combines with due concern for doctrinal requirements.

Special attention is given to the activity of the World Council of Churches, the Conference of European Churches and the Christian Peace Conference. Working actively in these world Christian bodies, representatives of the Romanian Orthodox Church make known the positions that guide Romanian contemporary theology in ecumenical and other problems preoccupying the world today. Plans are well underway to build in Bucharest an ecumenical center and a new theological institute.

As regards the relationship of the Romanian Orthodox Church with other faiths, mention should be made of the academic consultation between Romanian theologians and representatives of the Jewish Committee, held last year in Bucharest in the spirit of friendship, love and mutual appreciation.

Discussion Questions for Chapter 3

1. Do North American churches have needs similar to those leading West German Christians to establish the Kirchentag and Evangelical Academies? How are we dealing with our problems of bringing Christian influence to bear in our societies?

2. Do North Americans have the same difficulty in dealing with the changes necessary for Third World liberation and development as West Germans do?

3. Since North American churches are not tax-supported state or national churches, as many are in Western Europe, are they free of the bureaucratic tendency toward self-preservation? In order to better accomplish our mission, do we need to develop more lay-led, grass-roots communities, such as those developing in Western Europe and, even more rapidly, in Latin America?

4. Though North Americans live in a quite different society than East Germany, can we, too, learn from the "School of God" Bishop Schönherr describes? Can we learn the difference between Christian faith and civil religion, the value of more real community in smaller congregations or groups within congregations and how to "make peace" in both socialist and capitalist societies? Have we begun "peace education" in our churches as East German churches have? Can we rejoice in the growing freedom of the church in East Germany?

5. Do you think the average North American Christian would be astonished at the continued growth of the Roman Catholic Church in Poland? How do you explain it? How is the identification of the Roman Catholic Church with the Polish nation similar to our civil religion, and how is it different? Is it important that the church be strong enough to compete ideologically with the state?

6. Do you find it surprising that the Romanian Orthodox Church, according to Bishop Vasile, is both so concerned for its own tradition and so open ecumenically? What do you think North American churches might learn ecumenically from the Romanian Othodox Church?

4. The Struggle Toward Shalom

The Shalom Vision

This study seeks to see the complexity of Europe and its churches *whole* because much of the contemporary mission of these churches is to restore the wholeness of *shalom* to this divided continent and help heal divisions that Europeans have contributed to around the world. This vision of comprehensive peace has been articulated ever more clearly since World War II by the conciliar movements uniting European churches. On the one hand, this has meant deepening the biblical foundations of their theology through restoring to theological centrality the basic biblical symbol, *shalom* and, on the other hand, broadening the scope of their mission from parochial and national concerns to international and universal commitments.

Judaic-Christian life, both as personal existence and social history, is always shaped and sustained by visions of God's intention for the fulfillment of creation. The prophets of the eighth century B.C., especially, expressed a vision of *shalom* where the claims and needs of all are satisfied because of a fulfilled covenant between God and persons and nature. It is a vision of comprehensive community where "swords are beaten into plowshares" because "God shall judge between many peoples" (Micah 4) and bring "equity for the meek of the earth" (Isaiah 11). The fundamental meaning of "shalom" in Hebrew religion and culture is "totality" or "wholeness." It applies both to individual and communal wholeness.

Christian churches have not always realized how central this symbol of *shalom* is to the gospel of the New Testament, characterized as the "gospel of peace" (Eph. 6:15), and in which Jesus is identified as constituting "our peace" (Eph. 2:14-16). In Colossians, it is the "peace of Christ" that unites all Christians in one body (Col. 3:15). The peacemakers are among those whom Jesus called "blessed" (Mt. 5:9). The gospel at its very center announces that the *shalom* envisioned as God's promise for the fulfillment of human history has come into our history through Jesus Christ. Jesus, therefore, has been named with Isaiah's symbol of the "Prince of Shalom." Those who receive him as Savior and Lord understand their salvation as the gift of *shalom* and conceive their mission as helping create *shalom* in the new creation Christ is bringing into being.

The Conference of European Churches (CEC) has deepened its theological foundations by placing this biblical motif at its center. The Theological Preparatory Commission, working between the 1974 and 1979 Assemblies on the theme "Alive to the World in the Power of the Holy Spirit," included a chapter on "Stewards of Creation and Servants of Peace—in a Troubled World." It sums up their contemporary shalomic vision:

> Peace and life are indivisible. Since peace has become vital for human life in a technological age, we must live in a responsible way, seeking to understand the realities of the context of which we are a part and putting all our resources into the common effort to solve the problems which menace the human family today. In Europe, which has long described itself as a Christian continent though often taking unchristian ways, the task of the churches today is to identify the factors which produce and reinforce the destructive tendencies and those which arise from spiritual sources to counteract those destructive tendencies.[1]

After suffering the second world war fought on European soil in this century, the churches can now name as "destructive tendencies": idolatrous nationalisms, arrogant racisms, economic greed, class hatred and ethnocentric religions. All find their worst expression in war's violence. It is no wonder that at the Amsterdam Assembly constituting the World Council of Churches in 1948, their first ecumenical opportunity, they declared that "war is contrary to the

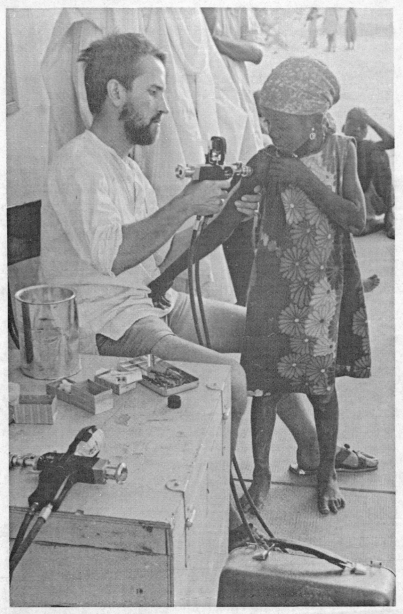

Agadez area of Niger. "Economic independence, sometimes expressed as the over-coming of neo-colonialism, is far from being accomplished, though the average European or North American has a hard time understanding why."

will of God." Since then, according to a CEC document, "the churches have worked together for peace and development at many levels in a spirit of ecumenical frankness which would have been inconceivable in 1945."[2] The growing solidarity of the churches in Europe, which they attribute to the work of the Holy Spirit among them, has made possible their growing contribution to peace.

Security and Disarmament

The churches of Europe have had a continuing ecumenical agency to deal with international affairs only after World War II. Between the two World Wars, the World Alliance for International Friendship played a pioneer role, but only as a loose association of national church committees. The Stockholm Conference of 1925 and the Oxford Conference of 1937 began to delineate the ecumenical responsibility of the churches in international affairs, but provided no structure for ongoing work. They thus were ill-prepared to make an effective witness for peace as the winds of change ushered in the whirlwind of World War II. Emerging from the destructive horror of that conflict, however, the churches needed no further convincing of the urgency of creating an effective, ecumenical instrument for peacemaking. A Conference of Church Leaders on International Affairs, meeting in Cambridge, England, August 4-7, 1946, wasted no time in projecting a commission to deal with this responsibility when the World Council of Churches would come into being in 1948.

Given the destruction of Europe, however, most of the resources for this enterprise had to come from England and North America. When the Commission of the Churches on International Affairs (CCIA) was formed in 1948, English was the mother tongue of 19 of the original 40 commissioners, as well as three of the four officers and seven of the eight staff members over the first 20 years of its existence. Consequently, the CCIA was not well-equipped to give adequate attention to European developments and problems.

On the other hand, a superb contribution to the agencies of the United Nations characterized the CCIA during the first two decades following World War II. This was especially true on issues of human rights. It was not as ready, however, to deal comprehensively with the new arms race, which was precipitated by the "cold war" and spreading across Europe during the 1950s and sixties.

Fortunately, during the decade of the seventies, CCIA leadership became more representative. Leopoldo Niilus of Argentina was chosen its director, and Professor Ulrich Scheuner of the Federal Republic of Germany, followed by Ambassador Olle Dahlen of Sweden, became chairpersons. By this decade the World Council as a whole also was more representative of the churches of the entire world, which meant that the CCIA had to turn its attention to a world wide range of issues, with an increasing concern for the "third world."

It was necessary and natural that uniquely European structures emerged in the 1950s to deal with the pressing European issues of security and disarmament. The preparatory meeting for the first assembly of the Conference of European Churches (CEC) in May 1957 took as its theme "The One Gospel in a Divided Europe," strangely similar to John Foster Dulles' address to the 1948 Assembly of the World Council titled "Christian Responsibility in our Divided World." But the content given it by these European Christians was starkly different; they did not see Christian faith as supporting any one side of this division. Speakers like Präses Michelis of the Evangelical Lutheran Church in Poland, Bishop Fuglsang-Damgaard of Denmark and Professor Roger Mehl of France addressed the need for East-West détente.[3] Seeking to remove "iron curtain" from Christian consciousness, Professor Andrew Ziak of Czechoslovakia urged banning this "expression of hatred."

When the Conference of European Churches met for the first time at Nyborg, Denmark in January 1959, at the height of the cold war, it spoke to the issue of security and disarmament:

> It is a task of the Church to pray and to work so that all atomic powers, under an effective international control, renounce the use of atomic weapons, and that the peoples of Europe and the whole world may be liberated from the threat of atomic war. Europe should serve as the basis for peaceful cooperation between peoples and not as the basis for the annihilation of life.[4]

This remained a topic of urgent and growing concern as the dangers of a nuclear-armed Europe escalated. By the time of the 5th Assembly in October 1967, CEC suggested what later emerged as the "Conference on Security and Cooperation in Europe":

> ... we suggest that there should take place a Conference
> of European heads of government. Such a conference
> would ... be a practical step towards the consolidation of
> peace. It could also play a significant part in the disappear-
> ance of hostile blocs, the deepening of friendly relations
> and the strengthening of cooperation in overcoming the
> tasks of development in the "third world."[5]

Committed to finding a new basis for European security, the CEC
organized a task force and consultation on "European Security and
the Churches" in November 1969 to deal directly with the political
responsibilities of the churches. Support grew for the political responsibilities of the churches and the processes negotiating the Conference on Security and Cooperation in Europe (CSCE). A new CEC
working group on "Peacemaking in Europe" was created in 1971
and held a major consultation May 28-June 1, 1973 in Switzerland on
the eve of the first meeting of the CSCE in Helsinki. The topic was
"The Consolidation of Peace in Europe: the Specific Contribution of
the Churches." Leaders of European churches judged the mid-
seventies to be a possible *kairos* in the biblical sense of a time filled
with new possibilities for God's intention of *shalom* in the world. In
this spirit, CEC welcomed the initiation of the CSCE and carried
through four "Post-Helsinki Consultations" (1975, 1977, 1978 and
1980) to help the churches mobilize support for its disarmament,
human rights, economic cooperation and cultural interchange dimensions.

The Christian Peace Conference (CPC), as already noted, emerged
at about the same time as the Conference of European Churches.
Based in Czechoslovakia, it was especially successful in mobilizing
the churches in the socialist countries of Eastern Europe to oppose the
Cold War and take responsibility for disarmament. In 1957, the very
same year that the preparatory meeting for the first assembly of CEC
also met, the consultation laying the foundation of the CPC convened
in Prague. Participants focused immediately on the danger of thermonuclear weapons for Europe and the world. Long before the partial
test ban treaty achieved in 1963, or the comprehensive test ban for
which we are still struggling, the CPC adopted as one of its first tasks:

> To condemn and reject atomic weapons, their use and
> even their tests, which are a threat to civilization and the

existence of mankind, and to make maximum efforts to ensure that atomic energy be used for the well-being of mankind.[6]

The theology articulated in the foundational meetings of the CPC saw these weapons of mass destruction as an offense against the goodness of God. Nothing could justify their production, testing or use.

Though some Christians in the West see the CPC as an instrument of communist propaganda or an East European attempt to split the ecumenical movement, it is in fact a cooperative part of the ecumenical movement. Motivated by its own authentic Christian inspiration, it emerged in the depths of the cold war to focus the task of the churches squarely on peace and especially on disarmament. Though the CPC must carry on its work within limitations established by communist goverments, and though that work was much disrupted by the Warsaw Pact 1968 invasion of Czechoslovakia, it has become a crucial center of contemporary peace action by the churches.

The Christian Peace Conference also has evaluated the CSCE-Helsinki Final Act as providing crucial possibilities for a new epoch in Europe and has rallied the churches to its support. It urges moving beyond political détente to military détente. The Disarmament Working Group at the 5th All-Christian Peace Assembly, meeting in Prague, June 1978, strongly supported the UN's Special Session on Disarmament in 1978, the SALT negotiating process between the USA and USSR, the reduction of conventional armaments in Europe being negotiated in Vienna and the release through disarmament of resources vital to economic development in the Third World.[7]

Despite the ecumenical peace action of the churches and many other peace forces, the arms race in Europe continued to escalate into the 1980s. In December 1979, NATO decided to deploy 572 new, intermediate-range cruise and ballistic missiles in Western Europe to counter the deployment by the Soviet Union of the mobile SS-20 intermediate-range ballistic missiles, which began in 1977. These new deployments increase the insecurity of all Europe because of the legitimate fear of both sides that a counter-force first strike capacity could destroy the other's deterrent force with almost no warning. Each side must keep its finger on a nuclear hair-trigger so that the missiles of the other side cannot destroy its missiles before they have a chance to fire.

It is urgent to get on quickly with the SALT process designed to negotiate the removal of the SS-20's in the east and reverse the decision to deploy Pershing II ballistic missiles and ground-launched cruise missiles in the west before their scheduled deployment in 1983. The ratification of SALT II and the rapid negotiation of SALT III have been at the top of the missional agenda of churches and church organizations in Europe.

In the light of these new east-west tensions, the Federation of Evangelical Churches in the German Democratic Republic recently defined "paths which the gospel opens" for political action:

> —of forgiveness, which makes possible one's own action and one's own first steps, even when they carry a risk;
> —of the privilege of encouraging others to a lack of prejudice, to openness, trust and sobriety in negotiations and conversations without worrying about ourselves;
> —of the reminder given with God's Word to view ourselves, the church and our own country critically;
> —of prayer, which, in the midst of all our activities, gives the final decision to God.[8]

May all churches east and west become increasingly faithful in the mission of directing themselves and their governments down these "paths" in the 1980s.

Holistic Human Rights

The excellent work of the World Council of Churches, and especially its Commission of the Churches on International Affairs, has been mentioned. Human rights is yet another dimension of contemporary mission in Europe and around the world where the ecumenical reconciliation of East and West is making an important contribution.

Following World War II the nations of the world reaffirmed their "faith in fundamental human rights" (Preamble to UN Charter). They defined as one of their principal purposes in the newly formed United Nations "to achieve international cooperation ... in promoting and encouraging respect for human rights and fundamental freedoms for all without distinction as to race, sex, language or religion" (Article 1, Section 3 of UN Charter).

The task proved more difficult than anticipated, however, because the United Nations has had to work with two human rights traditions. One, based in the democratic capitalist West, seeks to guarantee and protect personal dignity and freedom. The other is centered in the socialist East and focuses on the basic needs of persons to food, shelter, education, health care and work. The UN Commission on Human Rights, chaired by Eleanor Roosevelt in 1948, succeeded in uniting these two traditions in "The Universal Declaration of Human Rights." But drafting covenants of human rights that would become binding treaties the nations would sign and ratify proved more difficult, a process not completed until 1966. These two traditions now are articulated separately in the "Covenant on Civil and Political Rights" and the "Covenant on Economic, Social and Cultural Rights." Though most European states and Canada have ratified both, neither has been ratified by the US Senate, though President Carter finally signed them in 1977.

The WCC's Commission of the Churches on International Affairs has been active since its founding in the struggle to define and secure human rights. Professor Charles Malik of Lebanon, *rapporteur* of the UN Human Rights Commission when the "Universal Declaration" was formulated, was concurrently a commissioner of the CCIA. The first director, Dr. O. Frederick Nolde, had been executive secretary of the Joint Committee on Religious Liberty of the US Federal Council of Churches from 1943-48. In both his national and world ecumenical offices, he was a frequent spokesperson for the non-governmental organizations before the Human Rights commission. The CCIA, of course, had strong concern for religious liberty and the associated rights of freedom of opinion and expression, freedom of assembly and association, and the freedoms associated with family life and the education of children that make religious liberty meaningful.[9]

In its first decade the CCIA more concretely aligned Christian influence with civil rights relevant to religious freedom than with social, economic and cultural rights that claim justice in social existence. This tendency was deliberately corrected in 1972, however, when the Central Committee of the WCC, meeting in Utrecht, directed it to hold a Consultation on Human Rights before the end of 1974. It was to include men and women from all parts of the world, relate human rights concretely to cultural, socioeconomic and political settings of different parts of the world and pay particular attention to the needs of underdeveloped peoples. This kind of directive required broadening the earlier focus on civil rights to include social, economic and cultural rights.

The WCC's "Consultation on Human Rights and Christian Responsibility" met October 21-26, 1974 in St. Pölten, Austria. The 50 persons gathered from 34 countres moved toward consensus on a holistic understanding of human rights that sought to resolve the tension between civil rights and economic/social/cultural rights. They reported:

> Individual rights and collective rights are not in flat opposition. They are related. It should be the aim of the community to secure the welfare of all its members, the aim of the individual to serve the general good. In both instances, rights involve responsibilities.[10]

When the 5th Assembly of the WCC met in Nairobi, Kenya in 1975, the Helsinki Agreement on Security and Cooperation in Europe was affirmed as a "sign of hope in a world torn apart by opposing ideologies and divided by conflicting interests." In this agreement special attention was directed to the seventh principle governing relations between nations: "Respect for human rights and fundamental freedoms, including the freedom of thought, conscience, religion or belief." Alleged denials of religious liberty in the Soviet Union also received considerable attention. The Helsinki Agreement was seen as providing a new context and opportunity to deal with such human rights issues. The general secretary was directed to call consultations with the member churches of the signatory states of the Helsinki Agreement, and in 1976 and 1977 the CCIA did call such consultations in Montreux, Switzerland. A result was the decision to create the "Churches' Human Rights Program for the Implementation of the Helsinki Final Act."

Because the United States and Canada are among the signatory states of the Helsinki Final Act, this human rights program is co-sponsored by the Canadian Council of Churches and the National Council of Churches of Christ in the USA along with the Conference of European Churches. A working committtee has been created with eight members representing the CEC (four from Eastern Europe and four from Western Europe), two the NCCC-USA and one the CCC. A program secretary in the person of Dr. Theo Tschuy, a Swiss Methodist minister, has been elected. This is the first time joint action in any area has been attempted by these three councils of churches. The concern is to stimulate study and dialogue on the interrelation of the two human rights traditions represented in the Helsinki Agreement and act together in dealing with concrete cases of the violation of human rights.

To achieve this goal is both difficult and dangerous. The churches dare not allow themselves to become tools of ideological political forces. On the basis of their own faith and theology, they also do not dare ignore the suffering of those whose rights are violated, whether Blacks, Native Americans, undocumented immigrants in North America, migrant laborers in Western Europe or dissenting groups of Evangelical Christians, Baptists and Pentecostals in the Soviet Union.[11]

Moreover, the Helsinki Final Act has in some ways aggravated the problem because of the monitoring groups it spawned. By July 1980, 43 members of Helsinki Watch Groups in the Soviet Union had been either imprisoned or exiled. The churches therefore must move carefully but resolutely to witness for human rights. Their basis is their growing holistic understanding of the interrelation of thhe contrasting human rights traditions.

May the day soon come when reciprocal criticism through responsible dialogue may be a form of mutual service and not ideological conflict. The churches are contributing to this dialogue so that democratic, capitalist societies of the West will learn that civil rights have little meaning for those systemically excluded from their equally important right to adequate food, health care, education and work; and socialist societies of the East discover how better to actualize the civil, political and religious liberties enshrined in their constitutions but not yet adequately incorporated into their social and political processes.

Liberation and Development

Both the disarmament and human rights issues already discussed fall primarily along an east-west axis and require the churches' mission of reconciliation. Domination, dependence and development, which we will deal with now, are primarily north-south issues. They call for the churches' mission of liberation.

Willy Brandt, who contributed much to east-west reconciliation as chancellor of the Federal Republic of Germany from 1969-74, has from 1977-79 chaired an "Independent Commission on International Development Issues." The title of its report, *North-South, A Program for Survival*,[12] shows this new direction. In his introduction, Herr Brandt claims, "If reduced to a simple denominator, this Report deals with peace." Showing the relationship between the justice of a new economic order in north-south relations and the arms race that continues to aggravate east-west relations, he points to an interest shared by all: to avert the economic chaos that threatens our world on a massive scale if economic structures established after World War II are not modified.[13] The report following his words starkly outlines the predicament of the South:

> The nations of the South see themselves as sharing a common destiny. Their solidarity in global negotiations stems from the awareness of being dependent on the North and unequal with it; and a great many of them are bound together by their colonial experience. The North including Eastern Europe has a quarter of the world's population and four-fifths of its income. ... In the North, the average person can expect to live for more than seventy years; he or she will rarely be hungry, and will be educated at least up to secondary level. In the countries of the South the great majority of the people have a life expectancy of closer to fifty years; in the poorest countries one out of every four children dies before the age of five; one-fifth or more of all the people in the South suffer from hunger and malnutrition; fifty percent have no chance to become literate.[14]

The historical causes of North-South tensions also must be recognized. When the present international economic order was organized at Bretton Woods and, after World War II, through the United Nations, most of the present nations of the South were European colonies. (In 1946 the UN had only 55 members, while in 1979 this number had grown to 152. Beginning with India in 1947, most of those added were those who had gained independence from European colonial powers.) The World Bank and the International Monetary Fund, negotiated before the former colonies reached independence,

Bahati Martyrs Church in Nairobi, Kenya, holds three services every Sunday morning — one in English, one in Kikuyu and one in Swahili.

are therefore controlled by the major industrial countries of Europe and North America.

The United Nations has become the principal forum for these new representatives of the South. Its World Health Organization, International Labor Organization, UN Development Program, Food and Agriculture Organization, UN Education, Scientific and Cultural Organization (UNESCO) and the UN Conference on Trade and Development (UNCTAD) are among its instruments of development. Within them, and especially through UNCTAD, the poor nations of the South have been increasingly successful in moving the focus of concern away from only aid and technical assistance to structural reform of the world economic system. They thus hope to overcome the remnants of colonialism built into the present system and add economic independence to political independence.

Economic independence, sometimes expressed as the overcoming of neo-colonialism, is far from being accomplished, though the average European or North American has a hard time understanding why. With little comprehension of the structures left over from the colonial period, they too often blame lack of hard work and ambition. European nations did not colonize Africa, Asia and Latin America for the sake of the Christian missionary enterprise or to spread the enlightenment of European culture. The colonies were conquered and their economies reorganized to benefit the industrialized, northern states by providing them raw materials and markets for their manufactured products.

What this meant specifically was forcibly breaking traditional economies of subsistence agriculture and orienting them to the large scale production of export crops. In the process, of course, a transportation system of ports, railways, and roads was built, but primarily these were to facilitate international trade, not to meet the domestic needs of the people. In the course of the shift in the economy a structural dependence on the governing colonial powers was created. This dependency was maintained through control of all the financial institutions controlling the means of trade.

Many Third World nations of the South, who now depend on the world wide sale of their agricultural or mineral commodities, have promoted the idea of a "Common Fund." It would function as a public international bank and provide loans to producers that would enable them to stabilize the price fluctuations of the commodities upon which their economies are based. Such a program on an international scale is similar to the farm subsidies supporting the incomes of European and North American farmers. As yet, there is all too little readiness in the North to extend this benefit to the poor of the Third World.

In the light of this, it is not surprising that in December 1974 the Third World nations of the South led the General Assembly of the UN to adopt a "Charter of Economic Rights and Duties of States" to promote a new international economic order. A key sentence in its preamble is:

> *Declaring* that it is a fundamental purpose of this Charter to promote the establishment of the new international economic order, based on equity, sovereign equality, interdependence, common interest and cooperation among all states, irrespective of their economic and social systems ...

Though 120 states voted in favor of such an order (and only six were against and ten abstained), actual negotiations for structural change have moved very slowly.

What has occurred instead is a sharp decline in the percentage of economic aid given by the major western industrialized nations as they resist the structural changes pressed for by their former colonies in the Third World. Total aid as a share of the combined gross national product of the donor countries stood at 0.32 percent in 1979, far short of the target of 0.7 percent agreed upon in the UN in 1970.[15] Between 1965 and 1977, economic aid as a percentage of GNP declined in West Germany from .40 percent to .27 percent, in France from .76 percent to .63 percent, in the United Kingdom from .47 percent to .38 percent, and in the USA from .49 percent to .22 percent. In the OECD as a whole it declined on the average from .44 percent in 1965, to .31 percent in 1977. Fortunately, there are a few exceptions, with Canada increasing from .19 percent in 1965 to .51 percent in 1977, Norway from .16 percent to .82 percent, and Sweden from .19 percent to .99 percent. However, these commendable increases from societies with relatively small economies are not enough to offset the decreases in those with larger economies.[16]

No wonder the Independent Commission on International Development Issues chaired by Willy Brandt concluded:

> There must be a substantial increase in the transfer of

resources in developing countries in order to finance:
1. Projects and programmes to alleviate poverty and to expand food production, especially in the least developed countries.
2. Exploration and development of energy and mineral resources.
3. Stabilization of the prices and earnings of commodity exports and expanded domestic processing of commodities.[17]

Even more innovative and controversial is their proposal that some of these resources be raised by a system of "international levies" or taxes on such items as arms production or exports, international travel, international trade and the mining of minerals from the deep sea-beds of oceans.[18] The ecumenical church, with its global concern, can only be grateful that our international institutions are maturing toward the point where such suggestions may be considered feasible by responsible statesmen. It is also hopeful that leaders of the Soviet Union and East European countries, who have heretofore provided little Third World economic aid on the grounds that they were not their former colonies, assured the Commission that they took these problems with great seriousness and strongly favored changes in international economies and financial systems and institutions.

The World Council of Churches, with its increasing representation from Third World churches, is the ecumenical forum where European churches have dealt most decisively with the issues of the South's liberation from neo-colonial dependency. Its Central Committee, meeting in Geneva, July/August, 1977, adopted a "Statement on the New International Economic Order," which said in part:

> In 1974 the United Nations took a bold initiative to call for the establishment of a New International Economic Order. It emerged out of the recognition that the present order is unjust, discriminatory and disadvantageous to the poor countries which contain nearly two-thirds of the world's population.... The churches of the world should encourage reflection and discussion on the NIEO and undertake with renewed vigor educational programmes to build up awareness on the part of their constituency and the public

at large. The present unjust system will survive as long as people allow it to exist. A new and just order will emerge only if people are convinced of the required changes and their political backing is mobilized.

Active concern for liberation and development has characterized the WCC, especially since its Fourth Assembly in Uppsala in 1968. The Commission on the Churches' Participation in Development (CCPD) was established in 1970 to implement decisions made at Uppsala and the Consultation on Development Projects held at Montreux, Switzerland in January, 1970. It has carried on a vigorous program of study, experimentation, consultation and publication on these issues, with strong support especially from the churches of Sweden, the Federal Republic of Germany and the Netherlands. Significant work also has been done on a more inclusive ecumenical base through the Committee on Society, Development and Peace (SODEPAX), begun jointly by the WCC and the Pontifical Commission on Justice and Peace of the Roman Catholic Church in 1968.

Thus far the more specifically European ecumenical bodies have given second place to these north-south economic justice issues, with their major emphasis consistently directed to disarmament concerns. Usually they tie in with the need for a new international order stressing greater economic justice for the South with their support for disarmament. The Conference of European Churches has convened four post-Helsinki consultations since 1975. The third, held in Siofok, Hungary, September 26-29, 1978, united these two concerns under the theme "Security, Disarmament and Economics." Professor Gyula Nagy's comment in the "Introduction" to the report of this consultation is characteristic of the concern:

> Because of mutual fear and the international arms trade, there has been a six-fold increase in weapons spending even in the poorest countries in the last twenty years. Today even they spend approximately 50,000 millon dollars a year on weapons of destruction instead of rice, bread, hospitals and schools.
> According to a United Nations report, even a 5 percent reduction in world arms spending would be sufficient to release enough funds to eliminate the worst distress and

bring international economic aid to these countries up to
the level recommended by the United Nations.[19]

As the Christian Peace Conference has included more active participation from African, Asian and Latin American representatives in
recent decades, the concerns for liberation and international economic justice have become more prominent in its work. But here, too,
they remain secondary to the primary concerns for east-west political
and military détente and disarmament.

Structurally, the Conference of European Churches has moved to
relate itself directly to the WCC's Commission on Inter-Church Aid,
Refugee and World Service (CICARWS) by establishing an Inter-
Church Service Desk to cooperate with the Europe desk in
CICARWS. This connecting link is intended to enhance the mission
of European churches in working toward north-south economic justice. Given the economic possibilities, most of the development aid
raised by the European churches comes from western churches. The
churches of the Federal Republic of Germany have been an especially
generous source of funds for Third World development.

The churches of West Germany also have gone to some lengths to
influence their society to support a more just international economic
order. The Protestant group who sponsors the Kirchentag and the
Roman Catholics sponsoring in alternate years the Katholikentag,
co-sponsored a Congress on Development Policy in January 1979.
More than 800 participants from the social, economic and political
decision-makers of the country came together to dialogue on the
theme "Development-Justice-Peace." For four days the German
Farmers Association, the Association of Christian Business Execu-
tives, the leaders of the major political parties, labor union leaders
and others discussed conflicts of interest and common convictions.
The Congress culminated a two-year process of study and preparation. It remains to be seen whether a new level of consensus in this
pluralistic and economically powerful country will lead to a new level
of action. But no event of this magnitude has been sponsored by the
churches for the sake of a more just international economic order
anywhere else in the developed world.[20]

Western Europe has also had to cope internally with another aspect
of the north-south problem. During the last two decades millions of
seasonal and immigrant workers from less developed Mediterranean
Europe were drawn to the expanding industrial nations of Northern

Europe. The massive flow of uprooted people challenges the church's ecumenicity in a new way. The Orthodox from Greece found themselves displaced in predominantly Roman Catholic or Protestant societies; Roman Catholics from Southern Italy were confused in the overwhelmingly Protestant Scandinavian countries; Muslims from Yugoslavia and Turkey were dislocated in western Christian cultures.

The churches in Eastern Europe also are active in giving development aid. Because of the difficulty in converting their national currencies into western currencies, however, most of their aid cannot flow through ecumenical channels based in Switzerland and they have developed their own programs. The Lutheran, Reformed, Baptist and Methodist Churches in the German Democratic Republic, for example, have cooperated for 20 years in a program called "Bread for the World." During these two decades 450 consignments have been sent to over 60 countries, often through Red Cross development programs. In this way, both emergency aid and long-term development support are given. In the latter part of 1979, East German churches gave 500,000 marks worth of drugs, bandages, tonics and vitamins to the people of Cambodia.

The spirit empowering European churches in their mission to help bring economic justice and liberation to people long under European colonial domination may be discerned in the recent "Bread for the World" appeal to the congregations of the German Democratic Republic. In an ecumenical celebration on December 4, 1979 in the historic Kreuz Kirche (Church of the Cross) in Dresden, the call to give ended:

> We have all the peoples of the world in sight. They belong to us as brothers and sisters. As Christ has shared himself with all of us, so shall everything we have be shared with all (2 Cor. 9:13). We want to do and we must do whatever good we can.[21]

The long-standing divisions in Europe—and caused by Europe—are slowly and painfully being healed in the twentieth century. The Shalom of God revealed in Christ is restoring wholeness through east-west reconciliation and north-south liberation. The work is slow and the obstacles, great. But the structures working for comprehensive disarmament, holistic human rights and global economic justice and liberation are in place as they never have been before.

It may take 1000 years, as the tragic division between the Orthodox and Roman Catholic Churches and societies in Europe has taught us. But it is also true that such divisions are possible to heal. On the isle of Patmos, that biblical place of eschatological vision, official discussions of representatives of the Roman Catholic and Orthodox Churches, designed to heal a division reaching back to 1054, began in 1980. May they be a sign of *shalom* for the healing of the nations and blessing of the people of the whole of Europe.

Discussion Questions for Chapter 4

1. Would the mission of North American churches be strengthened if a biblical understanding of shalom *helped integrate their worship, evangelism, nurture and action programs?*

2. Why is it that North American Christians and churches take the Helsinki Final Act (CSCE) so much less seriously than many of our European sisters and brothers? Should our churches and the National Council of Churches devote as much time and money to military détente and disarmament as European churches do?

3. Do you think the United States has not yet ratified the United Nations covenants on human rights because we already have an adequate human rights tradition in our Bill of Rights and other laws? Or is it that there are social forces that oppose a more comprehensive understanding of human rights? What should the churches' attitude and action be? How can US and Canadian churches cooperate in the "Churches' Human Rights Program for the Implementation of the Helsinki Final Act"?

4. Can North American churches learn from European churches how to influence our society to support a more just international economic order? Can we use the "civil religion" as a bridge between the churches and society for the cause of global justice in a way that some European churches use their national church character?

Conclusion:
Beyond Pluralism
Toward Shalom

As readers complete this study they should know more about both the wholeness and the pluralism of European culture and churches. European national pluralism approximates North American ethnic pluralism and, in fact, is the source of almost all of it. Greater appreciation for the variety and vitality of the churches in North American communities should also result from this better understanding of their European roots. The major difference between European and North American pluralism is the age and strength of the "walls" that mark the dividing lines. What for North Americans are only ethnic differences are for Europeans national divisions marked by armed borders.

The dangerous ideological division between the liberalism of Western Europe and Eastern Europe's communism is buttressed by the 1000 years of religious and political history dividing Eastern and Western Europe. North American, and especially US, understanding of this division is severely limited because the major media sources fail to give an adequate interpretation of Marxism and the societies of Eastern Europe. There is some realism in North Americans' pride in being part of the most pluralistic society in the world, but the forces that interpret and manage this pluralism may severely limit the knowledge that might lead toward healing this dangerous division.

The churches of Europe, in spite of their national character, are learning ecumenically how to transcend their ancient nationalisms and, even more importantly, to penetrate this wall between East and West. The World Council of Churches, the Conference of European Churches and the Christian Peace Conference increasingly have devoted themselves to this mission of reconciliation during the last 30 years.

The ecumenical and peace movements within North American churches also have made progress toward such reconciliation but the civil religion of the United States blocks US churches from going very far beyond the national consensus for the purpose of healing the hostility of this division. The social and economic support of US churches is jeopardized if they are suspected of "undermining" spiritual support for the "free world."

North American churches therefore exercise nothing like the spiritual energy of European churches in supporting the Helsinki Final Act, military détente and disarmament. On these issues alone we have much to learn from European sisters and brothers. How is it that the Federation of Evangelical Churches in East Germany has a more active program of peace education for its congregations than most North American churches? What would happen if some of the spiritual energy used ideologically on East European human rights issues were transformed into The Churches' Human Rights Program for the Implementation of the Helsinki Final Act? Can capitalist and socialist societies learn to work together toward more adequate understanding of, and support for, human rights?

Both the similarity and difference between East European and North American churches should also be clearer as we conclude this study. Churches in North America and East Europe experience a clear separation between church and state in a way that many West European churches do not. East Europeans and North American churches have to rely on the free decisions of their people for their participation and support. For these reasons, the worshiping congregations of both churches experience a degree of spiritual vitality that goes far beyond that of the average West European church.

The great difference between East European and North American churches is that communist governments are officially hostile to religion, while the official ideology of US and Canadian governments is supportive. This means that East European churches carefully safeguard their traditions in relation to the state ideology and

"The churches of Europe, in spite of their national character, are learning ecumenically how to transcend their ancient nationalisms and, even more importantly, to penetrate this wall between East and West."

support the ecumenical struggle for peace and justice. North American churches, in contrast, often blend their theology with the civil religion, which keeps them at a greater distance from the ecumenical search for *shalom*

The civil religion of some West European churches, especially those in West Germany, was broken before and during World War II by the attempt of the Nazi government's ideological misuse of the state churches for its own purposes. In the 35 years since the end of the war, the churches in Western Europe have fashioned new instruments like the Kirchentag, Evangelical Academies, Taize Community, Kerk en Wereld, and so forth in order to exert a greater spiritual influence on the economic, political and social issues in their countries. From them North American churches can learn how to reshape critically the civil religion in accordance with the gospel, rather than passively reflect this civil religion in their congregations.

It may not be necessary to remove the national flag from the chancel as most European churches have, but it certainly is necessary to remove national idolatry from Christian hearts. Because the state and national churches of Europe once were in the greatest danger of such idolatry, they are better able to teach us how to deal with the political idolatries of our civil religion. After leading evangelistic campaigns in Eastern Europe in 1977 and 1979 and learning from Christians in those societies, Billy Graham wrote in *Sojourners* in 1979:

> There have been times in the past when I have, I suppose, confused the kingdom of God with the American way of life. . . . I especially was impressed with the concerns various Christians in Yugoslavia, Hungary and Poland expressed about peace. I believe their concern is genuine and they have something to teach us there.[1]

May we also be more willing to learn as the result of this "trip" to the churches in Europe.

NOTES

Preface

1. The same tendency may also be seen among scholars. As excellent a book as William Clebsch's *Christianity in European History* (N.Y.: Oxford, 1979) is, it is devoted almost entirely to the study of Christian life in Western Europe. One can learn much from it, but little about Christian existence in Eastern Europe.
2. Belloc is cited in Alfred T. Hennelly's *Theologies in Conflict* (Maryknoll: Orbis, 1979), p. 177, which analyzes the challenge of European traditions by Latin American theologians.
3. "Domination and dependence" are frequent themes in contemporary ecumenical discussions. See, for instance, *To Break the Chains of Oppression* (1975), which reports on a workshop of the World Council of Churches' Commission on the Churches' Participation in Development.

Chapter 1

1. See William Clebsch, *Christianity in European History* (N.Y.: Oxford, 1979) for a competent contemporary overview and interpretation of European history as Christian religious history, although it tells the story of Western Europe more completely than that of Eastern Europe.
2. An excellent resource for understanding the history and spirituality of the Orthodox Church is John Meyendorff, *The Orthodox Church: Its Past and Its Role in the World Today* (Pantheon Books, 1962).
3. Reliable and detailed information for the first 40 years of the churches' experience in the Soviet Union may be found in Walter Kolarz, *Religion in the Soviet Union* (London and N.Y., Macmillan, 1961). More recent data is found in *IDOC European Dossiers Two and Three: Church and State in Eastern European Socialist Republics*, 1976. Trevor Beeson's

Discretion and Valour: Religious Conditions in Russia and Eastern Europe (Fontana Books, 1975), written in cooperation with a working party of the British Council of Churches, is another excellent source of accurate information and honest interpretation, although informed by a more negative perspective on East European societies than I find justified.

4. IDOC Dossiers, *Church Within Socialism,* op. cit., p. 117.
5. Origen, *Against Celsus,* VIII, 75.
6. Heer, *The Intellectual History of Europe,* tr. Jonathon Steinberg, (Cleveland: World, 1966), p. 31.
7. A rich resource for understanding European church-state relations, especially in the modern period until World War II, is Adolph Keller, *Church and State on the European Continent* (Chicago: Willett, Clark & Co., 1936, published for the ''Social Service Lecture Trust.'')
8. This essay is published among other places in *American Civil Religion,* Richey and Jones, eds., (N.Y.: Harper and Row, 1974), p. 45-75; the sentence quoted is on p. 65. This whole compilation of essays is very instructive on the point so briefly raised in our text. Robert Bellah's critique of civil religion is especially important for our purposes.

Chapter 2

1. This story is recounted best in Giancarlo Zizola, *The Utopia of Pope John XXIII,* tr. Helen Barolini (Maryknoll, N.Y.: Orbis Books, 1978). The words quoted are found on page 4. Fifteen years later, Billy Graham's ''Prophesies'' also supported disarmament. See *Sojourners,* August 1979, p. 12-13.
2. Cyrus R. Vance, speech on ''The U.S.—European Partnership,'' before the Royal Institute for International Affairs, London, December 9, 1978, Bureau of Public Affairs, U.S. Dept. of State. Most of the other information on the European Community given above also comes from US Dept. of State publications.
3. Quoted in ''Economy, World,'' *1980 Britannica Book of the Year,* p. 325.
4. For further information and statistical use of this very important index see *The United States and World Development Agenda, 1977, 1979,* (N.Y., Praeger Publisher), pp. 147 f. in the 1977 volume, and pages 129 f. in the 1979 volume. The statistics that follow are taken from these two volumes.
5. Taken directly from data in *The United States and World Development Agenda 1979,* pp. 170-171.
6. Column by Alan Tillier, *Paris Herald-Tribune,* Nov. 25, 1979.
7. Ruth Leger Sivard, *World Military and Social Expenditure 1979,* p. 5. This annual publication, sponsored by the British Council of Churches,

Peace Research Institute of Dundas, Canada, and five U.S. organizations including the Rockefeller and Stanley Foundations, is a marvelous resource on the social costs of militarism.

8. *Ibid.*, p. 25.
9. *Ibid.*, pp. 8-9.
10. *Ibid.*, p. 25.
11. See the essay by Albert Keim, "John Foster Dulles and the Protestant World Order Movement on the Eve of World War II," *Journal of Church and State,* Vol. 21 No. 1 (Winter 1979), pp. 73-89.
12. See Ingo Roer, *The Historical Course of the Christian Peace Conference* (Prague, 1974), adapted from a dissertation presented to the Comenius Theological Faculty. The section on "The Christian Peace Conference and the Oikumene," pp. 59-81, is the most germane; the material cited is on pp. 63-65.
13. Many fruits have come from Professor Machovec's labors. Perhaps the best known of his books, and the most fruitful for Christians, is *A Marxist Looks at Jesus* (Philadelphia: Fortress Press, 1976). Peter Hebblethwaite's "Introduction" to the volume is also a good, brief introduction to Machovec's larger role in European Christian-Marxist dialogue.
14. Roger Garaudy, *From Anathema to Dialogue* (New York: Herder and Herder, 1966), p. 31-32. For those who wish to pursue further study of the European Christian-Marxist dialogue during the decade of the sixties, see the annotated bibliogrpahy of Ans J. van der Bent, *The Christian-Marxist Dialogue 1959-1969,* published by the World Council of Churches in 1969. The author is the chief librarian of the WCC. My friend, Professor Paul Mojzes, is also completing a manuscript, which will be the first comprehensive history of this dialogue. I am grateful to him for some of the factual material in my account. See also the studies published by the Lutheran World Federation in 1977, *The Encounter of the Church with Movements of Social Change in Various Cultural Contexts (with Special Reference to Marxism),* for later work on these issues.

Chapter 4

1. The Conference of European Churches published the theological preparatory document for their VIIIth Assembly under the title *Alive to the World in the Power of the Holy Spirit* in 1979. Professor Gyula Nagy, Director of Studies of CEC, while on leave from the faculty of the Lutheran Theological Seminary in Budapest, was the principal editor. The paragraph quoted is from pp. 78-79.

2. *Ibid.*, pp. 74-75.
3. Cited in a lecture of Dr. Glen Garfield Williams on "The Conference of European Churches and Questions of European Security," given at the Lutheran Theological Academy, Budapest, October 1978, pp. 3-4. I depend heavily on this lecture for this account of CEC's actions for peace in Europe.
4. *Ibid.*, p. 6.
5. *Ibid.*, p. 11.
6. Roer, *Christian Peace Conference, op. cit.*, p. 9.
7. Documents on the Vth All-Christian Peace Assembly (Prague, 1979) pp. 173-177.
8. "Declaration on the Current World Political Situation," Berlin, January 22, 1980.
9. This story is well told in the volume by O. Frederick Nolde, *Free and Equal* (World Council of Churches, 1968). See especially p. 38. The principal orientation to civil rights may also be seen in the documents collected in the booklet, *Religious Freedom: Main Statements by the World Council of Churches 1948-1975* (WCC, 1976) especially the first ten items.
10. *Human Rights and Christian Responsibility:* Report of the Consultation, St. Pölten, Austria, WCC: CCIA, October 1975, p. 2.
11. One of the useful tools in developing this comprehensive perspective on human rights is a volume edited by Erich and Marilyn Weingartner, *Human Rights is more than Human Rights,* A Primer for Churches on Security and Cooperation in Europe, Rome, IDOC International, 1977. The article by David Dillon on "East-West Church Dialogue Deepens Understanding," *New World Outlook,* October 1979, pp. 33-35, is also helpful, especially for North American readers.
12. Published by MIT Press, Cambridge, Massachusetts, 1980, and Pan Books Ltd., London, England, 1980. The Commission was formed at the suggestion of Robert S. McNamara, President of the World Bank, in 1977, and consisted of a majority of Third World members, with European representatives from France, Great Britain, the Netherlands and Sweden, as well as Mr. Brandt from Germany. There also were two representatives from the United States and one from Canada. This commission's report is clear, compelling and increasingly influential.
13. *Ibid.*, pp. 13-15.
14. *Ibid.*, pp. 31-32.
15. "Economy, World," *1980 Britannica Book of the Year,* p. 324.
16. *The Inter-Dependent,* September, 1978.
17. *North-South, A Program for Survival,* op. cit., p. 290.
18. *Ibid.*, pp. 27-28 and 45-46.
19. Published as Occasional Paper No. 11 by the Conference of European Churches, Geneva, 1979. The quotation from Professor Nagy is on page

6. The paper by Professor Jozsef Bognar, Director of the Institute for World Economics of the Hungarian Academy of Sciences, incorporated in this volume as Chapter 4, is a well-informed and able contribution to the churches' discussion from the standpoint of an East European academic leader. He concludes that, ". . . the menace to the survival of humanity and of the nations does not come today primarily from the neighboring nations or from the historically inherited conflicts, but from the extreme inequity pervading the globe, and from the over-exploitation of nature." (p. 58)

20. The speeches and reports from this significant congress are published in German under the title, *Entwicklung-Gerechtigkeit-Frieden* (Development-Justice-Peace), by the Kaiser Verlag, Munchen—Grünewald Verlag, Mainz, 1979, 412 pages.

21. *Methodist News from the German Democratic Republic*, January 31, 1980, p. 1.

Conclusion

1. Billy Graham, "A Change of Heart," *Sojourners*, 12 August 1979, p. 12-13.